Narcissistic

Abuse

Secrets and Answers About Narcissism to Find Out the Recovery of Your Relationship — A Helpful Guide to Be Codependent No More

MELODY ROMIG

Text Copyright © [Melody Romig]

Legal & Disclaimer

Table of Contents

CHAPTER 3

NARCISSIST'S PARTNER

CHAPTER 4

CLOSE A RELATIONSHIP WITH A NARCISSIST AND GET WELL AFTER BREAKAGE

CHAPTER 5

CODEPENDENCY

CHAPTER 6

CODEPENDENCY IN LOVE

CHAPTER 7

AFFECTIVE DEPENDENCE – HOW TO GET OUT OF IT IN 3 STRATEGIES

CHAPTER 8

HOW TO EXIT A RELATIONSHIP OF CODEPENDENCE (HEALING AND FORGIVENESS TRAUMA)

CONCLUSION

Introduction

Congratulations on purchasing *Disarm Narcissism and Codependency,* and thank you for doing so!

If you're in a codependent relationship with a narcissist, you may think that you know what the problem is. You think the problem is the narcissist—if they just changed their behavior, you could be happy again. This crucial first step in identifying the problem is where a lot of people go wrong. The problem is not the narcissist—the problem is that you are relying on the narcissist for your happiness and self-worth.

I have seen the same story unfold time and time again. My friend or family member tells me how their partner constantly makes them feel worthless. Afterward, they fire right back at their partner about all the things they should be done differently. After spending far too long in such a relationship myself, I understand the pain that one feels when the person you love make you feel so insecure. You love him/her, so his/her words mean something to you. Because of your love for your, they can hurt you more than anyone else can. Since I learned so much from being in this relationship and getting out of it, I started helping my friends with their own codependent relationships. The relationships usually had to end—but not always. The ones who stayed together saw their relationships change dramatically, and this isn't possible when you're with a true narcissist who refuses to admit their faults and make changes. The experience of leaving a codependent relationship and helping my loved ones out of theirs made me realize how much I could help people by writing a book about it.

We'll look at relationships with narcissists from every angle. The solution to getting out of this toxic relationship depends on what stage of codependence you are in, as well as the form that your partner's narcissism takes. No matter your individual situation, we will get to the root of the problem and put you on the path to be happy again.

You'll learn how to create your own self-worth—a sense of worth that depends on you, and not what your narcissistic partner thinks. You'll learn how to disentangle yourself from your partner's ideas of you and forge your own identity. These are the two steps to escaping the toxicity of a relationship with a narcissist. I can't tell you that following these steps will be easy, but following them is a whole lot easier than falling into unhealthy patterns with your narcissistic partner.

Once you have freed yourself from the power your partner had over you, you'll wish you had done so much sooner. You will feel reborn—like you can do anything you set your mind to. Right now, the negative labels your partner has given you are holding you back. The most damaging thing about the labels is that you at least partially believe them to be true. Your stage of recovery can be measured entirely by how much you believe these labels. No other measure is necessary to see your progress—this is because the *one* essential change you have to make is not accepting your partner's idea of you anymore. I told you that you have to forge your own identity and your own self-worth — these steps are necessary to make this change.

Once you have your own idea of who you are — once you already know that you are valuable — your partner's ideas won't matter anymore. You know yourself better than they do. They will try to tell you who you are, but it won't have an effect on you any longer. You know who you are. The person that your partner describes exists in their head and their head alone.

I am living proof that these two essential steps work. When I was codependent on my narcissistic partner, I went through a lot of pain by placing value on his words. It was not until I came to a clear definition of who I was — it was not until I knew my self-worth for certain — that my partner's emotional abuse didn't affect me anymore.

When my friends and family members saw that we ended it, they told me how different I seemed. They said I seemed calmer, smarter, and above all, more confident. My self-improvement can only be explained by the journey I took looking inward before I broke up with my partner.

My loved ones went through similar transformations. All of us knew ourselves before we entered these relationships—it was our narcissistic partners who made us forget what we already knew about ourselves.

I went through this journey myself, and I helped my closest people in getting through it. You are just able to change your situation. This book will tell you everything I learned from my own experience and from helping my loved ones through their experiences.

Since you have such a comprehensive resource available to you, you will be better equipped to disarm narcissism and codependency than we ever were. Read it to the end, and you will have all the knowledge you need to assert your independence and decide what to do about your relationship with a narcissist.

The longer you spend in this relationship, the harder it will be to get out of it. I am giving you all the guidance you need to understand how your relationship holds you back; I tell you just how you will separate yourself from your narcissistic partner and move on with your life. After you finish reading, you won't have any more excuses to stay in this toxic situation. You need to read it from the beginning to the end to find your way out. The longer you put off learning the dynamics of your relationship, the longer it will take for you to see the emotional damage it does to you. You don't have to waste time when it comes to escape the narcissist's trap. Remember that I have been where you are, and I know what it takes to move on. I also know that time is of the essence when untangling your emotions from someone else's. Keep reading now, and you'll have the right tools to break out of codependency before it's too late.

There are plenty of books on this subject on the market—thanks again for choosing this one! Every effort was made to ensure it is full of as much useful information as possible. Please enjoy!

CHAPTER 1

NARCISSISM

1.1 What is Narcissism?

Relationships with narcissists always follow the same basic pattern. When you fall in love, the narcissist tells you how special and irreplaceable you are, but then, as time goes by, they have nothing but criticism and demeaning language for you.

This sudden change came from the psychological disorder your partner has: it's called Narcissistic Personality Disorder. The disorder comes with two basic traits. (1) They need constant affirmation from others so they can feel happy, and (2) they lack the ability to empathize with other people. A person with NPD doesn't care when they hurt other people—they only care about themselves.

The word narcissism comes from the name Narcissus, the demigod from Greek mythology. He was a dashing young man—so many fell for him—but he always rejected them. When he rejected the nymph Echo, the goddess Nemesis punished him by leading him to a pool. Narcissus saw his reflection in the water and fell in love with it. When he figured out it was just a reflection, he realized his love could never be fulfilled and killed himself. The narcissist you know might not be foolish enough not to recognize their own reflection, but it's likely they are fond of mirrors. This is typical for people with NPD.

The psychiatrists James F. Masterson and Sandy Hotchkiss broke down the characteristics of NPD into what they called the seven deadly sins of narcissism.

1. *Shamelessness.* Unbothered by others' objections to their behavior, narcissists never admit to feeling ashamed because they need to maintain the aura of perfection. Some claim that narcissists can't feel shame—that may be true, but we can't really know how someone feels. The important thing is that their shamelessness prevents them from

admitting fault. If narcissists do feel shame, they deal with the feeling by pushing it away and pretending they are perfect.

2. *Magical thinking*. How can narcissists believe they are perfect? Shouldn't they see all the same flaws you see? The answer is that they use magical thinking to blame their flaws on circumstances or on others. They have *cognitive distortions* that keep them from seeing the truth. They also use *projection* to blame their own problems on you.

3. *Arrogance*. When narcissists feel their ego is threatened, they make themselves feel superior by putting down others.

4. *Envy*. Narcissists diminish other people's accomplishments, so they don't feel threatened by them.

5. *Entitlement*. Narcissists don't go by the golden rule of treating everyone equally; they think they deserve better treatment than everyone else. When you don't treat them as special, they take this as you questioning their superiority, and they get angry.

6. *Exploitation*. They use people to prop up their inflated sense of self-worth. In the narcissist's eyes, their friends and family are in a lower position than they are. No one can stand this treatment for long, so narcissists' relationships never last.

7. *Bad boundaries*. They only see people as an extension of themselves. They

don't see other people as having dignity or their own needs. Narcissists don't see the people in their lives as individuals but as part of themselves. When you stick around a narcissist, you are their *narcissistic supply*: the people that validate the narcissist's inflated idea of themselves.

Psychiatrists know of no cure for NPD. Neither medication nor therapy has been found to treat narcissism.

We don't know what causes NPD, either. Psychologists have been trying to answer this question all the way back to Freud. Some suggest that it is the result of parents giving excessive attention to their child, making the child see themselves as exceptional when they become an adult. Others suggest the opposite — that narcissists didn't have affirmation when they were children, and they try to make up for it by obsessively seeking self-validation as adults.

Psychiatrists have been done a lot of research to find out how narcissism works. Across many studies, they see a trend of self-regulation in narcissists. *Self-regulation* refers to all the ways narcissists try to make themselves feel exceptional.

The seven deadly sins of narcissism are a good summary of self-regulation. Narcissists' shamelessness is necessary because they have to see themselves as without faults—their magical thinking is necessary because they need a way to avoid seeing these faults and so on.

In a moment, we'll get into the differences between healthy and pathological narcissism, but for now, just understand that it's normal to have some degree of self-regulation. All of us want to feel good about ourselves, so we try to see things in a light that makes us look better.

One study showed this by looking at a group of narcissists and a group of non-narcissists. Both groups were given a task and then asked to rate their performance. Narcissists and non-narcissists alike rated their performance as better than it was, but narcissists were far more extreme in their exaggeration.

This study shows that all of us have some degree of self-regulation, but narcissists take it to extreme levels.

1.2 Types of Narcissism

There is a good level of narcissism that all of us should have. *Healthy narcissism* is having confidence, independence, and a strong sense of self-worth. *Pathological narcissism* is taking these traits too far. People with NPD (narcissists) put so much value on their own self-worth that other people don't matter at all.

Freud said that healthy narcissism is necessary for normal human development. A lack of healthy narcissism is called "echoism" according to the nymph in the Greek myth. Echo had no sense of self-worth whatsoever, so she was devastated when Narcissus, the only meaning in her life, rejected her. Most people find a good balance between echoism and narcissism.

If we don't have enough healthy narcissism, we won't protect ourselves against harm. Without healthy narcissism, we will hurt ourselves, protecting the things we love with no regard for our own well-being.

There is such a thing as "healthy echoism," too. As long as we have some healthy narcissism to go with it, healthy echoism makes us protect others out of our love for them, which can give meaning to our lives.

Pathological narcissists only protect themselves; echoists only protect others. Mentally, healthy people protect both themselves and others. They are both empathic and self-loving.

One way to understand pathological narcissists is to look at the healthy narcissism you have in yourself. You can imagine how taking your narcissism to an unhealthy level would be destructive.

For instance, you know that other people have different ideas about the world than you do. However, it can still be hard to understand how people can live, having beliefs that you sometimes find detestable. It's normal to feel this way, and it's an example of narcissism. It's just healthy narcissism, however. Even though you can't always understand people's beliefs, at the end of the day, you know that other people are individuals with their own ideas.

Pathological narcissists do not understand this. They can also feel shocked about what other people believe, but they can't step back and think, "People have all kinds of different opinions." To them, they are the only existing person, and other people are only extensions of themselves.

When pathological narcissists come across someone with differing views, they immediately try to change that person's opinions to match theirs. Different opinions are not acceptable, so they must be "fixed."

You are surely familiar with this kind of behavior after spending time around a narcissist. Pathological narcissists behave in ways to protect themselves just like we all do, but they take it to extremes. It may feel a little strange to look at the less extreme narcissism in yourself, but it helps you to understand where the narcissist is coming from. You have to imagine self-protection becoming the only factor in your decision-making.

As a healthy narcissist, you have your own version of narcissistic supply. You have relationships with people making you feel happy.

The narcissist you are with is the exception to this. They are in your life because you aren't a pathological narcissist. Narcissists are in your life because of your echoism — you care about them, as toxic as they are. With the narcissist, you allow your echoism to override your self-protection.

A person with healthy narcissism can end up in a situation like this. Sometimes, we let toxic people in our lives because our love for them overrides our self-protection. It's hard for most of us to cut toxic people out of our lives because we have empathy. Even though toxic people hurt us, we think about how cutting them out of our lives would hurt them, and that holds us back.

The biggest difference between a healthy narcissist and a pathological narcissist is this: a pathological narcissist never changes. If you don't leave him/her, things will stay just as they are now.

A healthy narcissist will change between self-protection and empathy depending on the situation, but a pathological narcissist will *always* choose self-protection. Having a stable relationship with them is impossible.

1.3 Origin of the Inability to Love of the Narcissist

That's why narcissists can't love you: they love themselves absolutely, and you don't even fit into the picture. If you stay with a narcissist, you are trying to make someone love you who never will. It's a hard pill to swallow, but the sooner you accept this fact, the easier your recovery will be in the long run.

You were probably charmed by your partner's confidence at first. Who isn't attracted to confidence? But the source of this confidence was NPD, so now is the time to break out of a relationship that will never be stable or healthy.

Sometimes, it seems like they do love you. Sometimes, they say they are sorry for how they treat you, even if they never change. They promise that they will change, but they never do that.

When you are codependent on a narcissist, the rare times that they treat you well will test you. You hold onto the hope that they are not set in their ways.

But Narcissistic Personality Disorder is a real mental illness listed in the Diagnostic and Statistical Manual of Mental Disorders, the book of psychological abnormalities that psychiatrists have been updating since the 1950s. No progress has been made in curing or improving NPD for those who have it.

Hoping that a narcissist learns empathy is the same thing as hoping that someone's diabetes will magically disappear. Neither is going to happen. There is no cure for either. And unlike diabetes, NPD doesn't only harm the person who has it: it harms all the people that have contact with it.

When a narcissist treats you well, it can seem like love, but they only look upon people favorably when they affirm their exaggerated sense of self-worth. They see you as a tool to confirm their self-worth and nothing more.

When everything is going their way, they might briefly treat you like someone would treat a person they love, but that is just because their uninterrupted grandiosity is putting them in a good mood.

Real love isn't this fleeting. Real love puts you through times that make you question your relationship, but in a codependent relationship with a narcissist, this is the norm, and the exception is the rare times that they treat you like royalty.

If you haven't been with a non-narcissist before, being with a narcissist will give you a warped idea of what love is. It makes you believe that love means enduring the emotional abuse of your partner 90% of the time and enjoying the contrasting 10% of the time that the narcissist is happy.

That 10% keeps you from breaking up with the narcissist. You think to yourself, "If I do what they say, these good times will last longer, and one day they won't lash out at me so much."

But the narcissist is impossible to satisfy. Even if you learn how to keep them happy more often, the times that they seem to love you are never about you, but them. They don't love you — they love the uninterrupted sense of self-worth that you help them achieve. Narcissists are neurotic, so no matter how good you get at helping them feel like a god, it is never long-lasting. They always find something that disrupts their ego. The only way out of this cycle is out of the relationship.

There is probably still something that you can't wrap your head around when I tell you that narcissists can't love. You are probably thinking about the beginning of the relationship when the narcissist seemed like a totally different person.

Back then, you didn't have to walk through a minefield to make them happy. Compared to now, they were tolerant of your flaws. You might wonder why you can't just fix whatever went wrong along the way and find a way to return to those days.

I have an answer for you. Even back then, it was not you who they loved, but themselves. Since you just met and you barely knew each other, the narcissist didn't see your flaws. They saw you as perfect (just like they see themselves), so they incorporated you into their perfect vision of themselves: they saw their ideal image of themselves alongside you, another exemplar of perfection.

Here is the catch. The narcissist didn't see *you the person* as perfect; they saw *you the accessory to their perfect self* as perfect.

Once they became familiar with your flaws, this threatened their perfect accessory. You were no longer a perfect extension of their perfect selves. As a result, their behavior started to change. They criticized you incessantly, trying to make you turn into the perfect accessory they saw you as.

Now that they know your flaws, there is no going back. It's impossible to become the ideal image of you that the narcissist sees in their head.

Even if it were possible, you don't want to. You want to be with someone who loves you. Narcissists only love the perfect extension of themselves that they see you as. They don't love your person. This is why they try so hard to fix you — so they can fix the part of themselves that doesn't fit with their flawless self-image.

The narcissist may make you feel good on the rare occasions during which you meet their expectations, but you can't confuse these happy times with love. It **might** be love, but it's not "love" for you — it's love for the pristine image of themselves that you are helping them maintain.

1.4 How to Recognize a Narcissist and How to Avoid It?

We have covered the basics of Narcissistic Personality Disorder, but you should also know some practical signs to look out for indications meaning you're dating a narcissist:

- *They curse a lot*. A study at Washington University of St. Louis found that narcissists use a lot more explicit language than non-narcissists.

- *They have been in a lot of relationships.* For the reasons we have talked about, no one can stand being with a narcissist for long, so their relationships don't last. But since the narcissist is so insecure, they always need someone to tell them how great they are, so they find someone else to fill this role pretty quickly.

- *They complain that they don't get the things they deserve.* Their sense of entitlement causes them to feel perpetually wronged for all the things they don't have. Narcissists aren't just striving for more like we all should — they believe the fact that they don't already have it all means they have been conned.

- *They treat people horribly and feel justified when doing it.* Narcissists know when they are rude or unpleasant, but they feel it is necessary because someone has wronged them.

- *They call people "stupid" a lot.* Narcissists think they are literally the smartest person in the world. If someone disagrees with them, they're stupid. To them, "stupid" seems to mean "doesn't believe just what I believe."

- *They are overly competitive.* When they win, they brag about it obnoxiously. When they lose, they claim that someone didn't play by the rules.

You can see how all these signs coincide with the fundamental characteristics of a narcissist. We know that we have to steer clear of people with these characteristics, so how do we do it?

Keep in mind that you don't only want to avoid narcissists in your romantic life but in all aspects of your life. You want to stay away from them at work, and you want to stay away from narcissistic relatives. Narcissists do the most harm in romantic relationships because they make you feel special just to hurt you in the end. But no matter where narcissists come into your life, they are toxic people. They are emotionally draining, and they make everyone uncomfortable.

You can have cover two bases to avoid narcissists before they can infect your life.

The first is simply avoiding them physically. You may think this is silly, but it is surprising how powerful social conventions are. If you as much as walk near a narcissist, they may take advantage of your politeness and approach you. When they start talking to you, you may want to leave, but all your socialization has taught you that walking away from someone is rude, so you can't get yourself to do it.

If you spot someone who you suspect is a narcissist, don't give him/her the chance to trap you in social convention. Take a different route to where you're going.

The second side to avoid narcissists is to be aware of the deceptiveness of charm. Even if you know better than to be schmoozed, the matchless confidence of a narcissist may draw you in. When they talk, you can't hear a hint of doubt or hesitation, and it makes their words sound very convincing.

You know why narcissists don't experience doubt. They believe they are perfect and that everything they do or say is perfect. That's why they sound so confident.

Don't confuse confidence with the truth. As convincing as the narcissist's confidence may be, the fact that the narcissist believes what they are saying doesn't mean anything.

Don't confuse niceness with goodness, either. Someone may be friendly, but it doesn't mean they're a good person.

This goes for non-narcissists, too. Of course, I'm not saying that friendliness is a sign of a bad person. Just keep in mind that there is usually no benefit to acting rudely towards people. If someone is nice to you, they could be a good person who is just being nice, but they could also be a bad person who wants to gain your favor. If you cover these two bases, you will be able to keep narcissists out of your life. Just avoid them physically, and remember that charm can be mean of manipulation.

CHAPTER 2

NARCISSISM AND LOVE

2.1 The Pathological Narcissist and Love

By now, you are intimately familiar with how narcissists behave in a relationship.

Narcissists talk endlessly about themselves, never giving you a chance to speak. They are avid fishermen — for compliments, anyway. Narcissists crave your compliments, and they are always looking for them.

These are just the harmless annoyances that come with a relationship with a narcissist. Loving a narcissist also means enduring their personal attacks. It means getting whiplash from their sudden changes in mood.

Narcissists are perfectionists when it comes to their distorted, flawless vision of themselves. They take the smallest problems and turn them into a referendum on their value as a person.

You ask them a harmless question, and they take it as a slight aimed at them. You could say, "Did you go to the store today?" and they might react with anger, demanding why you think they can't manage their own time.

Their mood swings might lead you to think they have bipolar disorder, but if you pay attention to what triggers their changes in mood, it's always the same thing. They see a threat to their perceived self-image, and it sets them off.

Before we know anything about narcissism, we see their rage totally differently. We think maybe they are stressed; maybe we should be more sensitive. As these patterns continue, we start to piece together the truth.

It's sad that there are people in relationships like this who don't ever get to the core of the problem. They blame themselves, thinking they are doing something wrong that triggers narcissist's rage. Even worse, they think this is just how relationships are.

Fortunately, you don't fit into either of these groups. You identified narcissism as the core issue, and you turned to books to learn about it.

There is a term for the situation that you are in—Narcissistic Victim Syndrome. NSV describes all the struggles people go through when they are socially involved with a narcissist.

The symptoms of Narcissistic Victim Syndrome include:

- *Gaslighting* - Narcissist makes you bring everything you believe in into question to the point of making you feel like you're going crazy.

- *Losing trust in loved ones* - Your partner might push you away from your friends and family, telling you that they are a bad influence. They do this to make sure they have more influence over you than anyone else.

- *Low self-esteem* - Verbal abuse from someone you love has a serious effect on your psyche. You start believing the awful things your partner says about you.

- *Lost sense of autonomy* - Because of narcissist's criticisms, you lose faith in your ability to make your own judgments. You rely on your partner to make your decisions for you.

- *Obedience* - Your partner only gives you one choice: to do just as him/her say. Since you don't want to risk your relationship, you follow their directions and avoid doing anything that might make them mad.

- *The idealization of the narcissist* - This is the symptom where a lot of victims get stuck. They buy into the narcissist's view of themselves, using magical thinking to see past the flaws.

2.2 The Trap of Lethal Love

You are reading to find a way out of the narcissist's trap, but there is no denying that it can be hard. It's hard because you still have feelings of love and attachment. But your partner benefits from your love much more than you do. They use your love to fuel their tower-high egos.

Your partner traps you with the 10% we discussed in Chapter 1. They make you feel miserable most of the time, but since their rare happiness gives you the hope that things will change soon, you don't want to leave them. You also don't want to leave them because you still feel attached.

Although you don't do it on purpose, by feeding the narcissist's ego, you are trapping them, too. They are addicted to your compliance with their control.

Others have written about the codependent relationship with a narcissist and said that you "enable" your partner when you stay obedient to them.

It's true that your obedience feeds into their sense of entitlement, but "enable" is not the right word here. Giving someone money when you know they will spend it on drugs is enabling, but obeying a narcissist is something different.

Saying you're enabling someone makes it sound like you're making it possible for them to do a harmful behavior, they wouldn't be able to do otherwise. But a narcissist will see themselves as the center of the universe no matter what you do.

When you obey them, it makes them less likely to lash out at you, but the behaviors and habits don't change. If you don't obey them, they will unleash their rage, but the behaviors and habits don't change. You don't "enable" a narcissist by obeying them; you just make your life a little easier in the short term.

Every day starts to revolve around appeasing narcissists. You're still attached to them, so you don't want to leave them. You live for the rare moments they are nice to you.

Affective dependency and codependency also play a big role, and we'll go in-depth on these ideas later. Basically, the thing that also makes you feel trapped in your fear of being alone if you break up, as well as your fear of what will become of your partner.

All of these obstacles seem to prevent you from leaving your partner. But before you reach the point where you consider your options, things seem fine. The codependent relationship with a narcissist tends to follow a certain pattern. Let's get into the stages of this unstable relationship and talk about how each one keeps us from doing what's best for us.

2.3 Stages of a Love Story with a Narcissist

It's impossible to be close to narcissists. They maintain an emotional distance from you so they can feel greater-than-human. They put you down in order to feel greater themselves. When you started seeing each other, and your partner told you how special you were, they only did it to get you to feed their narcissism. It's easier to see all of this after you've been through these stages a few times. Some call these stages the idealize-devalue-discard cycle. The "idealize" and "devalue" stages sound right, but "discard" doesn't.

Those who talk about the idealize-devalue-discard cycle assume that the narcissist casually breaks up with their partner. They say that once the non-narcissist partner is fed up with the narcissist's behavior, they tell them the truth about the ways the narcissist is affecting them, and then the narcissist breaks up with their partner because they will no longer be part of their narcissistic supply.

As we have discussed, the narcissist depends on their partner's narcissistic supply just as much as the non-narcissistic partner depends on their emotional support. If the narcissist "discards" their partner right after they open up about their feelings, it probably means the break-up was an emotional reaction.

That's why the word "discard" is so misleading about what this stage is. It makes the break-up sound so casual. It makes it sound like the narcissist isn't codependent on their partner themselves.

More often than not, narcissists realize they can't function normally without their narcissistic supply, and they desperately try to win them back. Narcissists will briefly revert to being charming in order to do this, and unfortunately, they often succeed.

Calling it the "discard" stage suggests that narcissist's partner is the only codependent one; it suggests narcissists don't need their partner as much as their partner needs them, so narcissist can safely break things off with no repercussions. We will go into great detail on codependence later, but just know that codependence in a narcissistic relationship is always mutual. Both partners are codependent.

The only thing the "discard" stage gets right is that there is a period of separation. We call this stage "the gap." When the narcissist wins their partner over again, this is "the return." Let's get into each stage and discuss why the non-narcissist makes the wrong move.

The Idealization

Idealization is where all the pain of this kind of relationship begins. In this stage, the narcissist incorporates you into their ideal image of themselves. That's why they treat you so well in the beginning. It's sadly ironic that the stage you have the fondest memories of is the one where the narcissist planted the roots of control over you. Once you fall for them because of how they treated you in this stage, you find it hard to let go of these memories. You think, "Those times were just as real as these bad times are now. Surely, there must be a way to go back."

But as I said before, there is no way to go back, the reason being that the narcissist only saw you as perfect when they weren't yet aware of your flaws.

This is where the trap of lethal love begins. If there were no good times for you to look back on, you wouldn't stay with this toxic person for so long. You end up spending more time thinking about how things could go back to those days than you spend feeling happy. Your happiest times in a relationship shouldn't be when you're looking back at memories.

When we say that the narcissist sets out a trap, it's important to clarify. Narcissists are not the diabolical geniuses they want you to believe they are. They set out a trap, but that doesn't mean they did so intentionally. What really happened is they saw you as perfect like themselves, and when, later on, you both saw each other's flaws, you got stuck on these old memories.

They didn't intentionally mislead you about what the relationship was going to be like. Like you, narcissists thought these good times were indicative of the future. Just the same, you fall into the trap of wanting them to see you as perfect again, and you try to become perfect for them.

It's important that we don't give narcissists too much credit when we objectively look at what happens in these stages. For the same reason, we don't want to give them too much credit by calling the "gap" stage the "discard" stage; we don't want to give them too much credit by saying they knew you were imperfect all along and were just manipulating you.

They really did see you as perfect, but you both fell into the trap of thinking this could last. Narcissists want you to think they are a mastermind when what they really are is a delusional, validation-seeking human being. Don't ever buy into their story about how amazing they are.

The Devaluation

One mistake people make when talking about devaluation is overestimating its consistency. They tell you that once you are in the devaluation stage, narcissists have stopped adoring you completely, and now they never treat you well.

This isn't the case, because of the 10% that they treat you well. It will vary case by case, but most of the time, narcissists give you positive attention 10% of the time, and that keeps you from leaving them too soon.

During devaluation, they don't stop being good to you completely, but it is the exception, not the rule.

In this stage, narcissists seem emotionally distant when they didn't before. The truth is that they were emotionally distant before — you never got emotionally intimate with them in the first place.

The only difference now is that you can notice the emotional distance. At this point in a relationship, you would expect to know more about their vulnerabilities and weaknesses.

But a narcissist never reveals these things because, in their mind, they have no weaknesses. If they are aware of any in the back of their minds, they push it far back.

If you are emotionally intimate with your partner, it is acceptable to talk about each other's faults from time to time and find ways to improve. But that is not how a narcissist goes about things at all. Anything negative they say about you is fair game, and anything negative you say about them brings out their bad side.

Because of the first stage, devaluation makes you want to "correct" yourself for your partner. Doing this is impossible because their expectations of you are impossible.

Once you have been devalued long enough, the next stage begins: "the gap."

The Gap

There is a good chance you've already tried to get out of the relationship and it failed. When we try to leave a narcissist the first time, it tends to follow a pattern. We have a fight with them, and it feels like the last straw. We tell them we are leaving.

Maybe the narcissist breaks up with you. It's important to note that they never do this because you don't fulfill their expectations — even though they get so mad about your faults that it might seem like they would.

But in narcissist's mind, your faults give credibility to their greatness. They can live with your flawed self as long as they can berate you for it.

What they can't live with is their own greatness being questioned. You don't even have to say that they have flaws. A narcissist will take anything you say as having this meaning, no matter how ridiculous it is.

Still, the more directly you question their superiority, the more likely they are to break up with you in the act of anger. In codependent relationships with narcissists, what usually happens is either the narcissist loses their temper, and they break up, or the non-narcissist comes to their senses, and they break up.

Even if narcissists put on airs like the breakage doesn't affect them, their narcissistic supply is severely threatened by it, so they will almost always try to get you back before you come to them.

When the non-narcissist initiates the break-up, they tend to make some consequential mistakes. They keep narcissist's contact in their phone, for one. They stay in the same social circle the narcissist is part of. They might tell the narcissist that they want to "take a break" instead of making their tone final.

The victims of narcissistic abuse might make these mistakes, not knowing they are leaving themselves vulnerable to being captured again. They might do it unconsciously, hoping that the narcissist rescues them from their loneliness, learns from the experience, and changes into a new person.

Whatever the victim's reason, they do not set themselves up for a real break-up, so they are setting the stage for more pain and abuse.

Later in the book, we will talk about the "no contact" method of breaking things off with a narcissist. But it is not only this method that makes it works — you will also have to use the space "no contact" giving you to reclaim your sense of identity and self-worth.

When you effectively break up with a narcissist, you have to reclaim what they took from you before you can emotionally move past your ex. Until you do this, you will end up back at the next stage, "the return."

The Return

Since we emotionally came to the decision to break up without first achieving our own sense of self-worth, we return to them.

Unless we know our self-worth, we feel like we are missing something when we are separate from the narcissist. In some cases, this empty feeling will cause us to go back to the narcissists after breaking up with them. But most of the time, they come to us.

If you come to the narcissist first, this is a sign that you have a long way to go before you can break out of this cycle.

But if that applies to you, don't lose hope. Think of it as a learning experience. Now that you know all about the toxic dynamics of a relationship with a narcissist, you are well-equipped to do better next time. When we get into codependence and affective dependence, you will objectively understand that angle of the relationship too. The more personal experience you have with the narcissist and the more you read about how their mind works, the easier it becomes to rid yourself of them.

There is an unfortunate number of blog posts that victims of these relationships will write, telling you how you can get narcissists to come back after they disappear. Some narcissists take pride in being able to get on without you, using other sources of narcissistic supply in the meantime.

But eventually, they try to chase you back down. Their new sources eventually get sick of them, and they try to get you back as a source.

This is why it's so important to cut off communication with them fully when you break up. No matter how much time has passed, they will eventually try to find you again. Since some of the bad memories have faded by that point, you might feel tempted to give in to their pleas.

Narcissists use specific techniques to win you back called *recapture strategies*. Read on to see what they are and how to be unmoved by them.

With that said, if the narcissist has found a way to communicate with you and employ their recapture strategies, that means you didn't do a good enough job to cut them out of your life. They shouldn't have the chance to pull these tricks on you in the first place.

2.4 Recapture Strategies

When your relationship starts back up again, the narcissist rewards you by treating you well for a short period of time. Soon after, things go back to emotional abuse. You aren't happy, but the narcissist is because they have their best source of narcissistic supply back.

For high narcissists is so important to have their egos validated that will say anything to get you back. Here are some examples of the recapture strategies they use to do it.

~

"We could try being friends."

This is rarely genuine even when the utterer isn't a narcissist. If a narcissist says this to you, they are definitely planning for friendship to turn back into a relationship again.

The line makes you consider their plea because you think that a friendship would have greater boundaries than a relationship. But narcissists don't know the meaning of boundaries. Whether you call the reignited engagement a friendship or a relationship, they will treat you the same.

Besides, you don't want to be friend with a narcissist more than you want to be in a relationship with them. Even if they give you more space (which they won't), in their eyes, you will still be the broken accessory that they need to fix. Don't give them this way back into your life.

"There are so many freaks out there. Stay with me because we know what we're getting into."

The old "stick with what you're familiar with" logic. Familiar Gaslighting, emotional abuse, bossiness, and personal attacks are hardly better because they are familiar.

"You don't seem like yourself. Let me help you feel better."

Your ex wants you to see being with them as a return to normality. But the truth is that it takes time to recover from narcissistic abuse, and the state of normalcy doesn't seem close until you spend a significant amount of time with the perpetrator out of your life. Going back to them would be the opposite of going back to normal. It would reset all the progress you made, forget about it!

This strategy also exploits your codependence on them. When narcissists say you don't seem like yourself, they are really saying, "If you took me back, you wouldn't feel so lonely anymore."

This person is not going to make you feel better. They will hurt you more if you give them a chance. Do not give it to them.

"I'll see a therapist."

You learned in the first chapter that medication and therapy have no effect on narcissism. Maybe if they did, the story would be different.

Besides, however willing they seem to improve themselves, they are only saying this to get back into your life. Every recapture strategy serves the sole purpose of getting you back.

Narcissists don't care if they are telling the truth or not. To them, the ends justify the means as long as you provide them narcissistic supply again.

"You put me through a lot when you left me."

A lot of recapture strategies rely on flattery, but some of them use guilt trips and threats. If you're still codependent on the narcissist, this line is very effective. Narcissists manipulate your emotions by playing to the empathy that they know you have. They know that you still see them as a person, and even more, a person you had a connection with.

It doesn't help that movies glamorize the idea of soulmates who can't stand to be apart. They make people think it is good to get all your emotional needs from one person. We gloss over the fact that Romeo and Juliet both died unnecessarily, each thinking the other was already dead.

These movies make people want to have their own relationships like these. When your narcissistic ex comes back and tells you all the pain you put them through, the movies make us think it's romantic to say, "I should never have left you. We need each other to be whole!"

You can find a healthy relationship that doesn't put you through so much pain. But you never need to be with one person to feel happy. When the narcissist uses this recapture strategy, they are counting on you to (1) feel bad for them enough to take them back, and (2) think you both need each other to be happy.

Don't fall for it. You've already been through a relationship with them before. You know that they don't make you happy.

You might object, "I'm not usually happy with them, but when I'm not with them, I'm never happy."

This is an issue we'll examine later in the book, but in the meantime, I want you to contemplate something. It isn't the narcissist that you are missing; it's the self-affirmation that they gave you.

Your partner doesn't do this job well most of the time; most of the time, they make you feel worse. Even if they weren't the worst possible person for this job — that is, a narcissist — no one person can do this for you. Your identity and self-worth have to come from inside.

This recapture strategy gives us a lot to think about because it gets to the heart of why codependent relationships don't work. Once you feel unmoved by this line, you are probably ready to move on with your life without looking back.

~

I have a special lesson to give you before we go to the next chapter.

You have to start paying attention to what you are teaching your narcissistic partner. I don't mean to teach as in teaching a school subject, but as in teaching a dog a trick.

It's a little odd to talk about people this way, but psychologists have done countless studies on how people learn, and it's not so different from how dogs learn tricks. The term for it is *operant conditioning*.

Humans learn that rewards and punishments are associated with different behaviors. As a dog learns that playing dead will get it a treat, a human learns that an apology will get them back in someone's life.

Teach your narcissist a new thing to associate with apologizing or using a recapture strategy. If their recapture strategy worked before, that means you taught them to associate the recapture strategy with having you back. Take a look below to get a clear idea of the analogy.

Dog

Behavior: play dead

Association: get a treat

Narcissist

Behavior: use recapture strategy

Association: get ex back

In both situations, you get to choose what happens as a result of the behavior. You get to choose the association the dog and narcissist make.

What association should you teach the narcissist? If there is something that narcissists can't stand — even more than their being superiority being questioned — it's indifference.

If you reaffirm narcissists' superiority, they are happy. If you question it, they blow up at you, but their distorted perception of self-worth remains. This is because, to them, yelling at you for questioning them keeps their distorted self-worth intact.

But if you act indifferent during a narcissist's emotion-laden speech to get you back, they won't know what to do with themselves. You aren't giving them narcissistic supply, but they can't get mad at you either, because you haven't done anything.

Eventually, they will learn that you won't give them any attention whatsoever. You stay silent and expressionless, no matter how ridiculous they act. This is the best way to get a narcissist to leave you alone.

Narcissist

Behavior: use recapture strategy

Association: silent, emotionless indifference

CHAPTER 3

NARCISSIST'S PARTNER

3.1 When the Narcissist Is a Woman

The motivation behind a narcissist is always to have power over their partner, and that doesn't change when the narcissist is a woman. A woman narcissist is, in most respects, the same as a male one. The main difference is that her gender role gives her tools of manipulation that a male narcissist would not have.

The most common example is female narcissist's sob stories. She told you early on how she was wronged, cheated on, and abused. Whether or not these events had anything to do with you is of no importance to her. Her sob stories make you want to treat her extra well. She takes advantage of that and gets as much self-validation out of you as she can.

When you don't meet her expectations, or you question her behavior, she uses tears to stop you.

When you display emotions, it's the opposite. When she says something condescending to you, you get upset. She uses your tone as an excuse to silence you. "You're inconsiderate!" she'll say. But her condescension was inconsiderate as well, whether she said it in an even tone or not.

Another tool the woman narcissist can use is her social role. This doesn't always apply when you're in a relationship with one, but she can take the role of the mother or the nice young woman and use it to protect herself from criticism.

Even when she doesn't have one of these social roles, a woman narcissist has to display a lot more abusive behavior until people call her a narcissist. Women are not who we generally think of when we think of narcissists. We might think of conceited divas or popular mean girls from high school, but these categories don't have quite the same connotation.

It's worth interrogating why that is — why is it that we hear the word "narcissist," a man is the first thing that comes to mind?

Psychologists have found that men are more likely to be narcissists, especially young men, so the mere fact that they are more common is part of the reason. This doesn't mean that women narcissists are especially rare, however. Men take up a greater proportion of the narcissists in the world, but they leave plenty of room for the equally toxic woman narcissists.

A second reason might be that we typically associate men with crime and other psychiatric disorders like psychopathy. To put another way, we usually think of men firstly when we think about bad things in society. On the other side of things, everyone has a mother, so we might have difficulty seeing someone like our mother being something as nasty as a narcissist.

We can never ignore the effect that mass media has on us, either. Several (unfortunately popular) TV shows focus on "genius" male narcissists. There is probably a show with a woman narcissist character, but I certainly can't come up with one at the top of my head. I can think about three male ones right away — House, Dexter, Sherlock. It wasn't even hard. Part of the reason we see narcissists as males might be these TV shows. (While we're on the subject, let's reflect on how male narcissists must idolize characters like House. Now that you know how people with NPD operate, it's easier to see these weaknesses.)

Those three factors may contribute to the fact that we associate men with narcissism more than women. None of this is to justify our prejudices. On the contrary, we should look at our prejudices directly and ask ourselves why we don't associate women with the label "narcissist" or other negative labels like "murderer" and "sex offender." If we don't acknowledge our prejudices, we won't have any luck fixing them.

Making the case that women can be narcissists might seem like a strange thing to do. It's not a label that anyone wants to be associated with (unless you are a narcissist, in which case it doesn't bother you). But we had to dive into this blind spot of our culture because men can suffer from the emotional abuse of a narcissist woman just as a woman can suffer from the abuse of a narcissist man.

Since I know men who have been with woman narcissist partners, I know for a fact that the narcissistic abuse they endure is just as serious. I have been mindful of this throughout the book; it's why I use "they" as a gender-unknown pronoun for the narcissist. The situation is mostly the same whether the narcissist is a man or woman, but there are still some unique aspects to the woman narcissist's abuse, as we have discussed.

It's particularly important to talk about this issue because many of the men who realize their partner is a narcissist feel like they can't ask for help the same way a woman can.

A close male relative once approached me, knowing that I had split off with my fiancé. He was light on the details (I think because of the stigma of men being victims), but he told me that his girlfriend might be a narcissist.

His girlfriend had many of the traits of a narcissist woman. She had a tragic backstory; she used tears to silence him; she was incredibly arrogant and materialistic.

Men can fall into a narcissist's trap of lethal love, just like women can. My male relative's girlfriend put him through the worst gaslighting I had ever heard of.

When she asked him at the beginning of the relationship, if he wanted kids, he said no. With her words, she seemed to confirm that she understood this. But every time they had sex, she would casually suggest not using protection.

When he said he wanted to use protection, that's when he saw a completely different side of her. She went on a long, emotional rant about why she couldn't be with a man who didn't want kids.

He told me this was only the first time. Everything seemed to cool down quickly, but then he made the mistake of asking her where she went when she came home. The question sent her into another loud rant about getting a prescription for contraceptives. This time she cried, and he felt obligated to tell her he would think about having kids.

From my relative's lived experience, you can see how a woman's narcissism can take on different forms from a man's, but all the fundamentals of a codependent relationship with a narcissist are still there.

He felt a *loss of autonomy* when she used tears to pressure him to have kids. If he couldn't be with her and make this decision for himself, then it wasn't really his decision. *Obedience* is also apparent in his story. She *gaslighted* him too, saying she accepted that he didn't want children at first, but then communicating the exact opposite in bursts of narcissistic rage.

It concerns me that many people would hear about his experience and immediately think, "Crazy, controlling girlfriend!" The "controlling" is part of it for sure, but what is going on here is much more specific than this outdated cliché.

Recall the two basic traits of someone with NPD. (1) A narcissist has an extreme sense of self-worth, and (2) they lack the ability to empathize with other people.

You could call his girlfriend crazy and controlling, but more specifically, she is a narcissist because she has both of these traits. My relative told me that she was constantly fishing for compliments. From her angry outbursts about wanting children, we can see that she couldn't empathize with him. Of course, the choice of whether or not to have kids can be an emotional topic that gets many people upset. But her attitude was the characteristic "my way or the highway" attitude that all narcissists have.

A woman's narcissism is not exactly the same as a man's, but it is mostly the same. The main differences are the tools that narcissist women use to manipulate their partners. They are certainly no less harmful than male narcissists.

3.2 Abuse of the Narcissist in Pairs

Another situation to consider is two narcissists in a relationship.

Narcissists gravitate towards each other. Psychologists say it may be because of other people are repelled by them. When two narcissists come together in a romantic pair, the resulting relationship is not so different from one with only one narcissist.

Like a relationship with just one narcissist, each partner makes the other feel worthless. They are both codependents on the other. Instead of the narcissist suffocating the other partner with talk about themselves, both narcissists compete for control. It's an equally unstable situation.

It might not be obvious at first that your partner is a narcissist, but it can also be less than obvious if you are a narcissist yourself. Narcissists don't come with a shipping label saying they are a narcissist, so sometimes it can be unsettling to think that you could be one.

Rest assured that you aren't a narcissist if you don't possess the two basic traits of

Narcissistic Personality Disorder. There is no need to overthink it and convince yourself you are a narcissist when you are not. This section only speaks to you if you do have an extremely high idea of yourself and you can't empathize with other people, and your partner exhibits these same traits.

To start, you should know that no relationship with a narcissist is healthy. If two narcissists are in a relationship together, two negatives don't make a positive like they do in multiplication. The relationship won't fulfill the needs of either partner.

Romantic relationships between two narcissists do have some unique characteristics that are worth covering if you find you are in this situation yourself.

Since narcissists are competitive, two narcissists in a relationship will always be trying to one-up each other. They can't do what other couples do and focus on their specialties ("I'm good at this; you're good at that"). Narcissists refuse to be anything less than perfect in everything they do.

You might think that two people competing with each other would be annoying for both parties, but not really harmful to the relationship. But when two narcissists have this mindset, and they are always together, it creates real problems.

Healthy couples have to collaborate to get by, not compete. If two narcissists in a relationship are always competing with each other to prove that they are the more competent one, neither will learn how to specialize in certain skills and leave the others to their partner. Since they are narcissists, both will believe they are great at every imaginable skill. In reality, though, neither of them gets good at any one skill because they're both trying to prove their superiority in every task.

The same idea extends beyond competitiveness. Beneath the surface of competition is each narcissist's fear that the other will discover they are a fraud.

The one-upmanship may seem like an inconsequential quirk of this relationship. To the onlooker, it is childish and unimportant. But to two narcissists engaged in a relationship, it is very serious. Every little household task seems to decide who the dominant one is.

Because it's no different when the relationship has two narcissists—the goal of each narcissist is the same: to assert power over their partner. When the narcissist's partner is a non-narcissist, this can be devastating for the victim, but from the narcissist's perspective, this is much easier. A non-narcissist who is won over by their charms won't challenge their sense of greatness.

Being with another narcissist makes things much harder. The other one doesn't simply accept their asserted power. They believe they are the ones deserving of control. The result is an unending contest for power.

It makes one wonder why a narcissist would enter such a relationship in the first place. Wouldn't they get along easier with someone who didn't challenge them so much?

You have to think from a narcissist's perspective to understand it. It's true that as a narcissist is buried deep inside their brain, they have doubts about their delusions of grandeur. But you could only find it by looking far into their unconscious. On the conscious level, a person with Narcissistic Personality Disorder is almost always certain of their superiority.

They might not seek out another narcissist intentionally, but narcissists have to believe this distorted idea of themselves in order to feel they are worth anything at all. If someone else with a high level of megalomania comes into view, the narcissist has no choice but to prove their own superiority. If they don't, they must be a fraud for sure.

Besides competitiveness, another challenge these pairs have is the difficulty of controlling another narcissist. At the beginning of the relationship, just like they would with a non-narcissist, a narcissist might easily incorporate this other narcissist into their sense of self. As it always goes, they find out that their partner is human, and everything changes. Both narcissists make the same discovery at some point, and both narcissists leave their partner because their superiority was directly questioned.

Up to this point, it can almost be seen as any other relationship with a narcissist. The same basic rule always applies, even in these circumstances: if the narcissists has their narcissistic supply, they keep up their delusional idea of their own self-worth. A relationship with two narcissists ends the same way as a relationship with one: the narcissistic supply that this partner provides is no longer any good, so they have to move on to another source.

There is one last thing to mention about the narcissist-narcissist relationship that we can apply to everything in this book. We haven't talked about it so far because it hasn't been relevant, but some people distinguish two kinds of narcissists. They say there are overt narcissists and covert narcissists.

The difference can be pretty accurately summarized as covert people having more introverted personalities and overt people being more loud and sociable.

We bring it up here because it can make a big difference in the narcissist-narcissist relationship. If one partner is covert and the other is the opposite, the overt narcissist tends to see their counterpart as the less dominant one simply because they are not as talkative. Meanwhile, the covert narcissist secretly believes they are the one in control behind the scenes. It is still a toxic relationship, as any relationship with a narcissist is, but it can last for a decent length of time because each narcissist can believe he/she is the one with the power.

CHAPTER 4

CLOSE A RELATIONSHIP WITH A NARCISSIST AND GET WELL AFTER BREAKAGE

4.1 Get Out of a Relationship with a Pathological Narcissist Using the "No Contact" Technique and the Process of Consciousness

Ending things with a narcissist will take drastic measures. The "no contact" strategy is just what it sounds like: after making it clear that you are breaking up, you tell them not to reach you, and you refuse to communicate with them in any way. This includes meeting them in person, calling and texting, and interaction over social media.

Because the narcissist depends on you to feel unique and important, they might disobey your wishes and try to contact you anyway — so you will have to block their contact on your phone and social media, as well as avoid them completely in the real world.

"No contact" is your only option for getting rid of the narcissist. If it is literally impossible for them to communicate with you, they won't be able to use a recapture strategy to get you back.

It is also a test of your own readiness to leave them behind. If you aren't ready to stop talking to them completely, then you are still not past the emotional side of the codependent relationship. You aren't ready to get on with your own life if part of you still thinks you need the baggage that your ex has become.

The "no contact" method is a necessary but insufficient step in stopping your narcissistic ex from infecting your life again. It's insufficient because it only handles the problem in the physical world.

In your mental world, you have to overcome your codependence by finding your identity and self-worth again. You have to do "no contact" first because you won't be able to reclaim your independence while the narcissist is still around.

It will start out like you are doing a juice cleanse. You will feel a rush of excitement when you realize everything about your daily life is going to change. You won't see this narcissist all the time anymore; they won't be a regular part of your life at all (if you follow "no contact" as you're supposed to, you won't see them at all). It's all right to savor this feeling while it lasts, but keep in mind that it doesn't last for very long.

I wish I could tell you that the separation is easy, but the truth is that after the rush of excitement comes a period of doubt and uncertainty. You wonder if leaving them was truly the right thing for you.

It is very similar to an addiction to a drug. Your relationship with them came with its own share of chemicals, like sex hormones and oxytocin, the chemical that your body releases when you touch someone.

But this isn't the only way it's similar. When you leave your ex behind for good, you still have to suffer some pain. Try to keep in your head that you would be feeling pain if you had stayed with them, too. The main difference between staying and the choice you made to leave is that you won't be feeling it indefinitely.

Pain and discomfort are part of life. You don't want to experience it too much, but sometimes, it is unavoidable. The best thing for you to do is to accept it.

There is no need for you to analyze the feelings you have. Emotions don't tell us anything on their own; they lead our thoughts into different directions, but on their own, emotions don't have anything specific to say to us.

Like dreams, they can let us know what we are thinking about on the deepest, most unconscious level. But emotions themselves do not have words for us. At the end of the day, you have to decide what you think and articulate it in your own words. The feelings that lead you that way are just vehicles. If you can't help but analyze what goes through your mind, analyze the journey, not the car you drive there.

In order to elaborate on the metaphor, emotions aren't traditional cars; they're more like self-driving cars that give you limited control. You can influence where you are going now and again, but not always. Sometimes, you have to let go of the wheel, lay back in your seat, and look out the window.

This is especially true when you feel your emotions strongly. You have no choice but to take the wheel if things go too far, but you usually don't have to do this. You are an adult with some life experience on your belt. Taking control will come naturally to you when it is necessary. So nothing is required of you to "prepare" for the emotional journey that the break-up will take you on.

Time passes on your occasionally turbulent car ride until, eventually, your emotions settle down. Your emotions might run high again for some time afterward, but it will never be as difficult as the first time.

If your emotions make you anxious during these hard times, think of how much better it is than the first time. It can be comforting to have a memory of when things were worse than you could refer back to.

The fact that your emotions were more exhausting in memory is also a reminder that things are getting better. You are starting to feel normal again.

Sometimes, you might wish you could just turn the pain off, but it is not an option. Since you have to feel it, you might as well feel it for what it is. Resisting emotional pain only makes it worse. As you feel whatever it is that you feel, you might have thoughts you might not otherwise have.

You might find yourself thinking that even in the darkest depths of your emotions, you are glad that you are finished with the narcissist.

It is a tremendous relief to lift such a heavy load off your shoulders. Be happy that you succeeded. Letting go of them was a hard road to take. You could have taken the passive road of letting your ex control your life, but you didn't let this happen.

You didn't accept codependence and devaluation as your reality. The narcissist had tortured you for long enough, so you faced the problem head-on and did what you had to do.

People in our lives have an enormous effect on us. They influence how we think about the world and ourselves. Over time, the people we see every day change our idea of what normal is.

When your life revolved around the narcissist, your normal was being demeaned and used. You couldn't allow this influence to be a normal part of your life any longer. You could feel the narcissist's poison rushing through your veins, and you had enough. Your narcissistic partner became your ex — you let the poison out of your body.

When we think about how emotional pain can be useful to teach us things, we should be sure not to glamorize it. As I said, emotions do not put words into things on their own. We do.

Sometimes, our emotions are just that — emotions. Whether you choose to overanalyze them or not, they eventually calm down. Brief but intense feelings are part of being human. Whatever thoughts run through your head while you heal from narcissistic abuse, the adjustment period of losing the person you used to love will not last forever. I'm trying to give you helpful advice on how to reflect on your emotions, but words are not always enough to tell us what to think or do.

In your healing process, there will be some things you will have to decide on your own. What will you learn from this time of transition? What thoughts do you have when you are not even trying to think deeply about these changes? Not every question has an answer. Not every emotion will make us ask a question.

I hope that my words have helped you, but you can't rely on one voice alone. What is your voice telling you? I'm sure it has some disagreements with mine. You should consult with your own voice before you follow through with anything I say.

After all, every victim of the narcissist was vulnerable to their exploitation because they had empathy. Unlike the narcissist, the victim was capable of seeing himself/herself in someone else. Narcissists took advantage of that and used this empathy to feed their narcissistic supply for as long as they could.

It's good to live inside another person's world from time to time, but you have to get out of it and live in your own world just as much. The more time you spend in your own mental world, the harder it will be for a narcissist or any manipulator to draw you into theirs. You will be able to use empathy just as well as before, but now, you will use it on your own terms.

When you spend time in your own mental world instead of jumping at every chance to go into someone else's, you give yourself a chance to find your identity.

In the introduction, we said that a strong sense of identity was necessary to lose the influence of the narcissist. The narcissist's idea of your identity is meaningless when you know who you are for yourself. We'll go deep into your identity near the end of the book.

To prepare yourself for this section, challenge yourself to spend more time with yourself. This means you don't distract yourself from the company of people or digital entertainment. Don't stress yourself out about doing this the right way; the challenge is very direct. Spend a few minutes with yourself, and pay attention to the thoughts that go by. This is the best way to get an idea of your identity. With practice, doing this goes from being intimidating to being relaxing.

We also said you needed a strong sense of self-worth to diminish narcissist's influence. It is closely connected to identity, but identity and self-worth are two different things. Your identity answers the question, "Who am I?" Your self-worth answers the question: "What good do I put into the world?"

You can focus on the moral angle of this question if you like, but don't limit your answer to that. You are part of the world, too. What goodness do you offer yourself? The world includes your loved ones and your community, too. What goodness do these people get from you? The world is broad and narrow. The "world" part shouldn't make you overthink the question.

Your assignment to prepare for our deep dive into self-worth is adding one small thing to the identity assignment. After spending some time with yourself, add more value to what you discovered about yourself. Sprinkle in some positive thoughts: "I really like watching comedies with my friend and laughing together." "The ritual of making coffee every morning can be so relaxing." The positive thoughts can be as random as these examples.

We covered a lot here, so feel free to take a break from reading if you need it. Until this chapter, we were laser-focused on the practical facts about narcissists and relationships with them. Knowing these things are necessary when you realize you need to protect yourself.

But it's just as important to learn how to approach the mental and emotional issues that come with disarming narcissism. You can't focus only on the practical information and science. You also have to make yourself mentally strong because narcissists play a mental game.

If you have your best cards in hand when your exes try to do mind tricks, you can't lose to them. You know all their plays. You are prepared for anything they try to do.

4.2 How to Heal After a Break-Up, and How to Have Conscious and Healthy Relationships

The "no contact" method is highly effective. It is like ripping off a band-aid. Still, there are necessary parts of the process you must endure. As with any break-up, no matter how strongly you feel you did the right thing, there will be a small part of you that misses how things once were.

As long as you don't forget your memories are more positive than what actually happened, and as long as you concentrate on re-establishing your own self-worth and identity, you will recover from the narcissistic abuse over time. As I have told you in the introduction, you will know you have fully recovered when their hurtful words don't mean anything to you anymore.

The healing that comes afterward will have you ready to find new love sooner than you think. With your narcissistic ex out of your life, it will be easy to see how much better your life is. You have already taken the poison out of your body. Now time has just to pass, and you will feel back to normal again.

You shouldn't have had to go through this in the first place, but if you can, try to find the positive out of it. One positive is that you learned something from experience.

But we already went over the mental and emotional aspects of the break-up. Now it's time to cover practical ways you can heal yourself after your ex is out of your life.

You will still have to overcome the emotional pain of letting go of someone you loved, and that's why the previous section talked about different ways you can think about the emotions you will go through.

There is no way we can simply skip this challenging step in the process. But we can contemplate what we went through and, as we are about to cover, make the transition period easier by following a few guidelines. If you take care of yourself using these practical tips, it will make getting back to normal a lot easier.

Take control of your attention. Ultimately, your attention is your life. If your attention is being spent on emails, social media, movies, pets, and so on, those things are what your life is filled with. By the same token, if your attention is being spent thinking about your exes, you are still letting them infect your life.

That said, it is always normal to think about them some of the time after breaking up. After all, they used to be a big part of your life. But now they aren't anymore.

It's time to spend your attention on new things. As long as they're not bad for you, you don't have to worry too much about what the new things are. You can buy plants to take care of, get into a new drama with hundreds of episodes, learn how to do something with your hands, and the list goes on.

As long as the new things taking up your attention aren't your ex, they will do for now. Eventually, you will be over your ex. The less attention they get from you every day, the sooner that day will be.

Cut out all the mutual friends you have with your ex. Psychologists say this is the best way you can ensure the narcissist doesn't find a way back into your life. I know blocking your ex was already hard enough, but they are addicted to the attention you give them, so they will find a way to corner you if you give them an inch.

If you have mutual friends who you really trust, then you might decide they are OK to keep. Otherwise, unfriend and unfollow the casual friends you have in common. The people you do keep, make it clear to them that you are going "no contact" with the narcissist. If you really do trust them, they will understand and won't interfere.

Let go of the shame. During the process, you might be hard on yourself to stay with the narcissist for so long. You might blame yourself for what happened. The best way out of this shame cycle is knowing it isn't factually accurate.

Reading this book is sure to make you realize all the factors that keep someone from breaking up with a narcissist. You were attached to them. They made you addicted to the rare times they treated you well. They manipulated you into thinking you needed them — and the list goes on.

What matters now is you found a way out of the trap of lethal love. You shouldn't be ashamed at all; you should be proud that you saved yourself.

If you follow these three guidelines, you will make the transition period as smooth as possible. Once you have moved on completely, you will be ready to find someone new to spend your life with. You will have learned all of the elements of an unhealthy relationship, so you won't let yourself make the same mistakes.

A healthy relationship is the opposite of a relationship with a narcissist. In a healthy relationship, you are both able to love yourselves and each other, not just the narcissist. You can talk openly about how you feel. Anything you felt you weren't allowed to do with your ex, you can do in a healthy relationship.

A codependent relationship with a narcissist is the opposite of a healthy relationship, so looking at the innate problems of your previous relationship is a good way of learning what a good relationship is.

There is another thing to keep in mind, though. The characteristics of healthy relationships are not so different from one kind of relationship to the next. Your relationships with friends, family, and co-workers all follow the same basic principles. The main difference between them is the part of ourselves we reveal in one relationship that we don't reveal in others.

I make a point to say this because thinking that your relationship with your significant other is dramatically different can have devastating consequences.

If you believe it's good to feel depressed when your partner is away, your partner and you are not independent enough. No matter how close you are to someone, you shouldn't feel broken when they aren't around. This is codependency, and it is not healthy in any situation.

Before proceeding to the chapter on codependency, here are the traits of a healthy relationship:

- You *don't* need each other to survive. Each of you could function on your own. This isn't to say that you wouldn't miss each other when the other is away or grieve if the worst happened, but that you can continue on despite these feelings.

- You take differences in opinion and values as a given. Of course, if you choose someone to be with, you probably have a lot of things in common, including your views on the world. But even so, it's inevitable that you disagree on some things.

- Both of you keep relationships with your families and friends. You can't rely on one person for all of your emotional needs. Fulfill your emotional needs by maintaining multiple healthy relationships.

- You can speak your mind without fear that your partner will threaten to break up with you. Ultimatums like that are common in relationships with narcissists. Don't be with someone who would do that again.

- Be willing to compromise. It's a cliché, but a true one. You can't expect your partner to do just as you say all the time, but you can meet them in the middle. This way, your partner feels like you are considering their autonomy, and they are more likely to do it.

Each characteristic of a healthy relationship has one thing in common: they require that each partner is independent and emotionally mature. It's no wonder narcissists, and healthy relationships don't go together.

In other words, having a healthy relationship requires each of you to be the opposite of a narcissist. Don't always be fixed on your own needs; consider your partner's, too.

Both of you have to do this for your relationship to work, but if you find an independent, emotionally mature person, it is possible. No relationship is easy, but they don't have to be hard, either. Keeping them healthy takes work and empathy.

CHAPTER 5

CODEPENDENCY

5.1 What Is Affective Dependence? What Is Codependency?

When two people are codependent, they are dependent on each other's dependence on them. People in a codependent couple *needs their partner to need them.*

When a codependent couple is apart, their emotions go haywire. They can't function normally without the other. They obsessively worry if their partner is doing all right. If you are codependent, you are either spending all your time with your partner or worrying about him/her. You hardly spend time doing anything else.

It's clear why narcissists thrive in codependent relationships. Their partner doesn't want to leave their sight, so they can serve as the narcissist's constant source of self-validation. Narcissists is codependent because they *need you to need them* so you can continue to provide narcissistic supply.

Narcissists' partner is codependent because they know, on some level, that their partner needs narcissistic supply in order to feel happy. But at the early stages, they don't know narcissistic supply is what they give their partner. They think it's healthy and normal for a couple to need each other so desperately.

It's often confused with codependency, but affective dependence is something different. It is when you depend on one person for all your emotional needs.

Narcissists seek out someone who they deem to be insecure so that they won't leave them. You depend on the narcissist for all your emotional needs, while the narcissist takes advantage of this and depends on you for narcissistic supply.

There is a big difference between what the narcissist and you are doing, even if you are both affectively dependent. Narcissists intentionally find someone with low self-esteem who can keep up their massive ego. You, on the other hand, did not seek out narcissists to take advantage of them. You were just looking for the same emotional support everyone needs.

Yet the narcissist and you made the same fundamental mistake. You tried to find affirmation in another person, which is ultimately unsustainable. The only thing you can find stable affirmation in is yourself.

5.2 Which Individuals Are the Most Suitable Subjects to Live in Codependent Relationships?

Codependency isn't limited to relationships with narcissists. It happens any time one partner needs constant attention, and the other tries to satisfy their insatiable needs.

The dynamics play out when one partner is a *people-pleaser,* and the other is focused solely on their own needs.

You can see how narcissists fit in the framework of codependency, but the same dynamic happens in relationships with drug addicts and alcoholics. The people-pleaser thinks they can fix their partner.

The "taking" partner never changes, but the people-pleaser stays with them because of the 10% of the time they see a ray of hope. The alcoholic, drug addict or narcissist will promise they can change, and the people-pleaser clings onto that hope. The promise is never followed through, though.

Remember when I told you before that the narcissist is also codependent. Whether the people-pleasers partner is addicted to substances or themselves, they actually see their partner as a gleam of hope themselves.

As long as their partner is with them, they think their lives aren't empty. They try to fill this emptiness with alcoholism or drug abuse, but they never feel satisfied. They try to fill this emptiness with their partner's attention, too, but it is equally ineffective.

People-pleaser's partner doesn't act like the people-pleaser gives meaning to their life, even though they depend on them just as much as they depend on their substances or their obsession with themselves. This is because, like the people-pleaser, they depend *completely* on their partner to fill their emotional needs.

Depending on one person to make you happy never works, so they are caught in a cycle of expecting the people-pleaser to fulfill them, and always being disappointed.

It isn't the people-pleaser's fault that they can't make their partner happy, even though this is what they always think. Nobody can make someone happy on their own. The people-pleaser has tasked themselves with a job that is impossible to do.

The people-pleaser doesn't have an unlimited amount of energy that would be required of them to meet their partner's needs. The longer they stay with their substance-abusing or narcissistic partner, the more drained they feel.

They also feel resentful. They put their whole selves into making their partner happy and never seem to get anywhere. Then, the 10% happens — their whole lives center around fixing their partner, so they delude themselves into thinking they have succeeded. Things go back to how they were before. The cycle continues.

By staying in a codependent relationship with a narcissist, you are taking the "people-pleaser" role. The phrase has a negative connotation, even though it shouldn't.

It just means that you see the potential in people that others might not see. This is a great quality to have; you don't have to feel ashamed of seeing the good in people.

You can have this quality without letting people taking advantage of you. Breaking up with the narcissist doesn't mean you have to become cynical about people, thinking all of them will use you. There are people out there who could use someone like you in their lives to remind them they aren't stuck the way they are.

Narcissist is a different story, however. No matter how much you try to change them, they will stay the same. They will keep hurting you.

Narcissists have a serious psychological condition. Not even a doctor of psychiatry could change them. Since you are the kind of person who can see the good in people, you thought you could make them change their ways. But trying to make a narcissist change is a fruitless endeavor, and making yourself a part of their life will put you through long-term emotional pain.

Everyone has flaws; there is someone out there who would benefit from someone like you who can tell them the potential they have. There are people you can love and

help who won't take advantage of you for
it.

5.3 Could You Be Codependent?

You might want to think of yourself as
independent, so you probably don't want to
think of yourself as codependent. But ask
yourself: do you feel uneasy or less-than-
whole when your partner isn't around? Do
you worry that your partner can't get by
without you?

If your answers are "yes," you are
codependent. Don't worry about this too
much; people escape from codependency
every day, and you will too.

People who are codependent on their
partners put their all into the relationship.
You make sacrifices, barely thinking of

yourself, so that you can make your partner happy.

Your partner gives you nothing in return. They don't acknowledge the emotional labor that you do for them.

This causes the codependent partner to feel like they are trapped. Since they see so many stakes in making their partner better, they don't feel like they can just leave them behind. But even when they do their best to satisfy their partner, it is never enough. The partner taking advantage of their codependence gets as much out of your emotional labor as possible — in the case of the narcissist, using it as narcissistic supply.

Being with a narcissist means doing everything you can to keep their narcissistic supply flowing at all costs.

Narcissist's partner completely loses themselves in making sure this happens.

To put it crudely, some would say that the codependent partner is clingy. They never think or talk about anything besides their partner.

Even if you have exhibited some of these traits yourself, you can probably think of someone like this. It is pretty normal for us to be clingy with our partner early in the relationship, but when you are codependent for long periods of time, this is a sign that it is not a healthy relationship.

When you're with a narcissist, you're trying to extend their happiness as much as possible, and avoid their narcissistic rage as much as possible. These jobs are incredibly taxing; they don't leave you time or energy to do anything else.

It's not even that you have nothing to think about besides the narcissist. You simply feel like if you don't keep them happy, you can't be happy yourself. They don't give you a choice.

Earlier, we said that the people-pleaser personality is more vulnerable to falling into narcissist's codependent trap, but it doesn't take any special kind of person to become codependent. It can happen to anyone. It all depends on the stage of life we are in.

Even a relatively self-centered person can become codependent on a narcissist if they are really attached to them, and if they are chasing down their memory of what being with them used to be like.

With all this talk about codependency, it's very important you don't lose sight of the fact that codependency is a two-way street.

You may be codependent on your partner, but they are equally codependent on you.

It might not seem this way when they give nothing in return for all you do for them. But narcissists are codependent on you because they think you would be lost without them. They are so certain of their self-worth that they think their mere presence keeps you happy.

5.4 Correlation Between Narcissism and Codependency

The dynamic between a codependent person and a narcissist is often described as a dance. The narcissist becomes enamored by their partner's inclination to follow the way they move. The codependent partner is enamored by how the narcissist moves so boldly and leads them through the dance.

This stage of the dance doesn't last long. The codependent does want narcissists to consider their own feelings and tries to push them into this direction. The narcissist is upset that their partner has stopped doing just as they say.

Codependency and narcissism complement each other this way. They both end up resentful.

In real-life terms, narcissists want their partner to reaffirm their idea of reality. Their idea of reality is a fantastic one where they are the hero who does no wrong; they only do what is best for everyone.

The codependent partner is the opposite. They look to the narcissist to get their assessment of reality. Am I saying the right thing? Am I doing the right thing? While the narcissist depends on their partner to validate their exaggerated sense of self-worth, the codependent partner depends on the narcissist to evaluate their idea of the world. They are always changing their ideas of the world based on what the narcissist is telling them. From both sides, you can see how the narcissist is in control, and their partner gets pushed aside.

While you are certainly a victim when you are with a narcissist, it's important to understand your participation in the codependent relationship.

When you stop your half of the narcissist/codependent dynamic, you can see whether your partner has it in them to change. If they aren't a pathological narcissist, they will take it to heart if you tell them they have hurt you. If they project all the blame onto you, they are a pathological narcissist, and there is no chance of them changing.

As the codependent partner, especially as the unstable relationship goes on for longer periods of time, you feel a sense of commitment to the project of your partner. You feel proud that you keep them happy as much as you do. This is textbook codependency because your idea of self-worth depends entirely on how another person feels. A narcissist needs an impossible level of attention and care to feel content, so they need their partner to be codependent to get their narcissistic supply filled. You add fuel to narcissist's idea of themselves. You feel you don't have another choice because if you don't, you will face their rage. But codependency is what causes you to get stuck in this cycle. If you weren't codependent, it would be clear early in the relationship that you should break your ties with the narcissist. Until you realize you are codependent, and that being codependent is not a healthy feature of a happy relationship, you keep sourcing their narcissistic supply.

As a people-pleaser, you feel fulfilled when you pour all of yourself into making someone else happy. The codependent partner lives vicariously through the narcissist who they keep happy.

But even with this giving personality, you have limits. You become increasingly frustrated with your partner's behavioral patterns; no matter how much you follow their rules, nothing changes. Since narcissists find out that the relationship is not going to be as blissful as it was in the beginning, they become frustrated with the state of affairs too. Neither of you wants to break up because you both cling to the security and familiarity you get from the relationship, no matter how unhappy it makes you. You are afraid of being alone. You feel certain it would be worse than what you are going through now.

CHAPTER 6

CODEPENDENCY IN LOVE

6.1 The Characteristics of Conscious Relationships

You are more than capable to create a conscious relationship, but you will have to unlearn everything you learned from your narcissistic ex.

As a conscious partner, you will ask your S.O. (significant other) if anything is bothering them. In return, you should feel free to tell them about what troubles you.

We went over the characteristics of a healthy relationship, but a conscious relationship is a different thing. A conscious relationship is certainly a healthy one, but when your relationship is conscious, it means that you are ready to hear each other out and improve yourselves. You can see how this would lead to a healthy relationship.

A conscious relationship has these characteristics:

Effective Communication

A conscious relationship doesn't mean that you don't tell each other how you feel. In a relationship with a narcissist, it seems like you have to hold back what you feel so you don't set your partner off. But in a conscious relationship, both partners are able to tell each other how they feel.

This is not to say you can say just what is on your mind with no filter. You still have to be mindful of your word choice and think about how your words will sound to your partner. But you don't let this keep you from expressing yourself.

It goes the other way, too. You have to make it clear to your partner that they can be open with you. You tell them directly with your words that they can be open with you, and you tell them with your actions that they can be open. If you tell them in words that they can be open, but then you shoot them down every time they try to express themselves, you are telling them to keep their thoughts to themselves. Never forget that effective communication requires each partner to be an active listener.

The most important rule to follow in achieving effective communication is sticking with "I-statements" and never using "You-statements."

If your partner is doing something that upsets you, don't say, "You are driving me crazy watching TV all day." Tell them, "I think it would be nice if we did something together instead." "I-statements" take all of the accusations out of your tone and make for more effective communication.

Above all, show your partner that you are willing to negotiate with them. If you act like an authoritarian partner, they will stubbornly ignore you.

If you make it clear that you hear their own concerns, they will be more willing to hear yours.

Honesty

In terms of a healthy relationship, honesty means improving your communication with your partner, as we just illustrated. But in terms of a conscious relationship, honesty goes deeper.

We are speaking of *internal* honesty. Have you accepted your partner's flaws? Have you accepted your own flaws?

When you are codependent on a narcissist, you create an idealized portrait of them. You don't allow yourself to see them realistically. In a conscious relationship, both partners have to be aware of their significant other's weaknesses as well as their own.

Being honest about your flaws doesn't mean you have to accept them. When we say you accept your flaws, we only mean acknowledging them. If you can embrace each other's flaws, with active trust, you can work on them together.

Active Trust

This characteristic isn't a good one to have in a relationship with a narcissist. When you are always choosing to take a leap of faith for a narcissist, they will let you fall to the sea every time.

But after you spend some time dating and you find someone who you think is worthy of your trust, active trust is a necessary ingredient in a conscious relationship with them.

The closer that you get, the more times you will see them fail to meet your expectations. As long as they don't make any mistakes that are worthy of losing them, you need to have active trust in them so they can improve.

If you change your assessment of your partner from "perfect soulmate" to "unreliable train wreck," every time they make a mistake, you'll never find anyone who makes you happy. It's partly about forgiving them for their mistakes, but it's also about being aware of how they rely on you.

If you find someone worthy of it, take a leap of faith when they try to better themselves.

If you never believe in them, they won't feel motivated to get better.

Active trust is also about seeing the gradients in trust. There are a lot of degrees of trust between "blind trust" and "no trust."

When you find someone new after losing the narcissist, you will be very good at picking up what traits make a good life partner. There is a very good chance you find someone with real potential to spend your life with.

Now you just have to unlearn what the narcissist taught you. They taught you to trust them completely the 10% of the time they treated you with respect, and not trust them at all when they didn't.

Narcissists keep you on this emotional rollercoaster to keep you off balance and ultimately control you. The partner you have after the narcissist will be capable of having a conscious relationship. You will respect each other enough to know the other is worthy of being trusted even after they slip up.

6.2 The Daily Habits of a Conscious Partner

In this book, we tackle the question of what makes a conscious relationship from two sides: the principles of a conscious relationship and the actions we take. We just learned that effective communication, honesty, and active trust are the basic tenets of a conscious relationship. What actions do we take to build these tenets into our daily life?

They are daily habits because we have to get into a routine of doing them every day. One of these habits is *telling your partner the negative emotions you are feeling*.

This habit encompasses all three tenets. It requires effective communication because you have to express your feelings in a constructive way; it requires honesty because you can't repress the feelings you have; it requires active trust because you need to have faith that your partner won't snap at you for telling them how you feel.

Oftentimes, you will notice that when you express your feelings early before they build up into something extreme, they are not as bad as you made them out to be. It truly helps to talk them out with your partner and see them for what they are.

Thoughts and feelings we have in our heads are almost always worse in our heads than they really are. When we keep them to ourselves, we make them into something they're not. That's why it's important to talk about our feelings with our partners — it diffuses the feelings that would otherwise come out in unconstructive ways.

When our feelings are more significant, our partner can help us work through them. You have someone you trust, so you might as well let them help you through difficult emotions.

Conscious couples also make a habit of *supporting each other in their dreams*. Your partner's dreams are ultimately theirs to see through, but having the support of their partner goes a long way in motivating them.

When you're with a narcissist, there is only room for your partner's dreams. In a conscious relationship, you can both pursue your dreams and remind each other what you are striving for.

Sometimes, life gets in the way, and we lose sight of our dreams. As conscious partners, you can remind each other that you want more out of life. Don't let your partner forget their dreams.

It's important that you find an empathetic partner who cares about your dreams, too. When you support them in their dreams, it will make an empathetic partner want to support yours as well.

Tell them directly what your dreams are; don't feel embarrassed about having dreams. All of us have them. Dreams are what keep us waking up every day. They make us happy because we know that our lives could be so much more.

When you think your partner's dream is out of reach, you have a few choices for how you want to approach them about it. If you can think of a way to communicate to them that they should shoot for something smaller first, this can make them feel like you are upfront with them, without making them feel like you don't believe in them.

For example, if your partner wants to be a stand-up comedian, don't just tell him/her to give up. Do research on open-mic nights in your area. Tell them instead of starting big and not knowing where to begin, sign up for one of these events, and feel it out.

Supporting your partner in their dreams is part of what keeps your relationship exciting. We all need to think the future could be better. Keep each other thinking your dreams could come true while also making sure the steps you take to get there are actionable and realistic.

Conscious couples give each other time and space to be alone.

You don't have to make a lot of fuss about wanting alone time. Working days are a natural time to have space away from your partner. Make sure you have things to occupy you that have nothing to do with your lover.

You had activities that made you happy before you met each other. Some of them are things that your partner wouldn't enjoy, so it's OK to do them yourself while they are somewhere else.

When you see your partner busy with something, you should leave him/her alone. Your lover would enjoy your company too, but later.

Having alone time is important because it allows us to reflect. Even when we are around people we really trust, the social expectations that come with someone else being in the room are more limiting to our reflection than we realize. The presence of other people unconsciously makes us censor our thoughts.

Besides that, other people are simply distracting. Being alone allows our thoughts to flow uninterrupted. We have to give ourselves and our partner time for this each day.

Alone time is not the only thing you have to fit into your routine. Conscious couples also *make date night a priority*.

Date nights remind you why you are together. They are periods of time where you can focus on just each other and not on the other things happening in your life.

If you keep busy schedules, put an event on your calendars to go out once a month, minimum. If you find yourselves without anything urgent to do one evening, be spontaneous and spend a night together in town. Unplanned nights out make some of the best memories.

Conscious couples *touch each other*. This includes but is definitely not limited to having sex. Not everyone likes to be touched all the time, but a simple touch on the shoulder can communicate your love for someone more than words can.

Study after study shows that happy couples touch each other more than unhappy ones. When you are touched, a hormone called oxytocin rushes through your body. This chemical is strongly linked to happiness.

Touch might not be a good idea when your partner is stressed or tense, but when you see that they are doing relatively fine, take the opportunity to hold their hand and tell them you are glad to have them. It sounds corny, but your lover will appreciate it.

Conscious couples share household work.

One of the main things couples argue about is who does the household labor. I am not going to tell you how your work should be split up — what matters is you both have a constructive conversation about it and agree on who does what.

You might come to an agreement that one person does more because the other is busy at work, but even with an arrangement like this, the working partner has to have tasks of their own. This is because household work makes you feel partially responsible for the state of your home.

If you do everything and your partner does nothing, they will end up taking everything you do for granted. Even a few simple chores will make your partner feel they have a stake in making your house a home.

This last habit is the most important out of all of them. It is the most difficult to master. Conscious couples *resolve conflicts*.

Notice we said plural "conflicts." We phrased it this way because you have to resolve each conflict individually without making each one decide the fate of your relationship.

Conscious couples are committed to solving problems; they don't assume their partner is fully to blame for every conflict, and they don't assume each conflict is a sign of a larger issue.

Embodying the characteristics of conscious couples makes resolving conflicts much easier.

When you embody *effective communication*, you tell your side of the story using "I-statements," not letting the argument spiral into an emotional fight by provoking your partner's defensiveness. "I-statements" help your partner understand your concern objectively.

Honesty allows you to express your feelings properly. If you censor yourself, you won't get to the root of the problem. Honesty also helps you see through your partner if you have a feeling they aren't telling you everything.

If you get that impression, don't make accusations. Just keep it in mind and ask them more about their side of the story. If you communicate with each other without letting your emotions overtake you, you will get to the bottom of the conflict.

The active trust will stop you from jumping to conclusions about your partner. You will try to see the best in them, and you will forgive them when they don't match up to your expectations.

To develop the habits of a conscious partner, you have to respect your significant other's autonomy, as well as recognize your own.

Keeping up a conscious relationship requires self-improvement, not partner-improvement. You couldn't change the narcissist, and you can't directly change anyone else, either.

What you can do is work on yourself. If you do this, your partner will feel free to be themselves and be inspired to improve themselves.

We are affected by the people we love more than we realize. When we spend time around someone who embodies these habits and characteristics, we start to change ourselves.

6.3 How to Overcome the Fear of Being Alone

It's possible that what worries you isn't finding a healthy relationship, but finding one at all. As you search for someone to spend your life with, remember that being in a healthy relationship is not so different from being alone. Either way, you need to learn how to live without needing another person.

The term for fear of being alone is autophobia. Interestingly, breaking down the word into its parts, autophobia actually means "fear of the self."

This is fitting because people with autophobia are not really afraid of not being around others. They are afraid of having to face themselves. People with autophobia prefer to have someone near them who can cover up the inner voice that they fear.

Even someone in an abusive relationship with a narcissist will stay with them because of their autophobia. They are unhappy in the relationship, but they are so afraid of being alone with themselves that they keep the narcissist in their life.

But you are not stuck with these two options: being with someone who doesn't love you, or being stuck with yourself. The fundamental reason you don't have to fear yourself is that you are never actually alone.

The thoughts in your head are not something to fear. Every single one of them came to be because of some influence in your life.

It isn't always easy to track down where our thoughts originated from, but if you pay attention to a single one and reflect on it deeply, you realize it never came from you. It came from something your friend told you; it came from something you read in the news; it came from an old memory of your childhood.

You are afraid of being alone because you are afraid of facing all the thoughts in your head. But your thoughts aren't anything to be afraid of. They are nothing more than fragments of memories. And none of them came from you — they came from another person out there in the world. This is why you are never really alone.

Sometimes, it seems like our thoughts are trying to push us in one direction or the other, but it only seems this way because our brains are constantly making connections. The human brain is constantly trying to tie loose ends and help things make sense. As a result, we are sometimes misled to think that our thoughts mean something when they don't.

This isn't to say your thoughts don't matter. They certainly do, but *not every single one of your thoughts is important*. In fact, the vast majority of them are completely inconsequential. There is no need for you to pay attention to all of them.

We aren't done talking about the mental side of achieving independence from your ex; in the next chapter, we'll put your mental independence to the test. You won't be able to finish this book without knowing you are free of autophobia.

Before we move on, there is another thing to consider on the subject of being alone. If you stayed with a narcissist for a long time, it is pretty likely that you have some level of autophobia, but it might not be the case for you.

Maybe your fear of being alone stems from the basic human need for companionship. It is perfectly natural for you to want people in your life who are close to you, especially a romantic partner whom to spend your life with.

The good news is that independence is a quality that many people look for in a life partner. By learning how to be happy with yourself, you make yourself a more attractive candidate for marriage and courtship.

You will crave someone to fill the void the narcissist used to fill, but you will have to learn these lessons of the self before you can find someone else to fill that role better.

6.4 How to Overcome the Fear of Being Alone

Since you were in a codependent relationship with a narcissist, you might be concerned that you aren't capable of being in a healthy one. Like I said in Chapter 4, the fundamental characteristics of these healthy, conscious relationships are honesty, effective communication, and active trust. These couples can talk openly without fear of repercussion, and each partner can hold their own when they aren't around their other half.

You already know you won't make the same mistakes with your next partner. If you were going to make the same mistakes, you would have stayed with the narcissist and kept on the path you were on.

But you left them. You already made a clear choice that you weren't going to let someone use you again.

And now you know what a healthy relationship will be like. You know it from this book, and you know it because you already participated in a relationship that was the opposite of a healthy one.

The contrast between your next relationship and the one with the narcissist will be at the forefront of your mind for a long time. The advantage of this will be that it will keep you on the right track; it will keep you from repeating the same mistakes.

The disadvantage is that you might get carried away by your fear of repeating the same mistakes. A lot of people who broke up with narcissists worry about this because they think they are a special kind of person who attracts narcissists.

After what you go through, and after reading this book, this is not something you will have to worry about.

Narcissists are drawn to people with low self-esteem and people-pleasers. You don't have to stop being a giving person to avoid narcissists, but you will know from experience that people can take advantage of it.

After practicing the techniques that we have gone over in this book, you won't have to worry about low self-esteem attracting narcissists, either. You will be certain of your self-worth, and that alone will keep narcissists at bay.

But sometimes, a person's fear of engaging in a relationship isn't just a result of being hurt by a narcissist. Sometimes, they are afraid of what it would be like for someone else to really get to know them. They are afraid that if someone got to know their true selves, they wouldn't want to be with them anymore.

It's undoubtedly true that the closer we get to people, the more they can hurt us. After leaving a narcissist, you are all too familiar with this fact.

But we can't let this fear of being hurt keep us from forming new bonds. If you meet someone new, they get to know you better, and then they lose interest, it's their loss.

Countless people are out there searching for someone. Soon enough, you will meet someone you are compatible with, and you will totally forget about the ones who passed you over.

You might be afraid of finding someone new because you are afraid of the pain you would feel if you break up. But now that you know what a healthy, conscious relationship looks like, you won't become codependent again. You will have your own identity, self-worth, and independence separate from your partner. If things don't work out, you still have all the things that matter most.

6.5 The Desire to Please and Be Loved at All Costs

When you were with the narcissist, you were willing to do whatever it took to get love from him/her. You made narcissist's happiness the center of your life.

When narcissist was happy, you took it to mean that he/she loved you. Now you know that this was not a sign that narcissist loved you, but that you were helping your narcissistic lover keep up his/her distorted self-image.

You lost yourself in making someone else the center of your life. It gave your life meaning to make the person you idealized happily.

Part of what kept you from leaving was the fear of losing this meaning in your life once they were gone. Even if you found someone to build a stable life with, you worried that you would lose the fulfillment of making the narcissist happy. In a twisted way, the fulfillment you got out of giving your narcissistic partner supply was something meaningful to you, even though part of you had to admit this wasn't how love should be.

When the narcissist was happy, you took this as meaning he/she loved you, and you specifically. Then, when your relationship fell apart, you came to find out that your partner could get his/her supply from anyone. They preferred you since you were such a reliable source, but if you weren't perfectly compliant with their wishes, they would find someone else to sustain their ego.

Outside of a relationship with a narcissist, you have to be careful not to fall into these patterns. You can still make someone else's happiness a determinant of your own even when your partner isn't a narcissist.

All you have to do is follow the characteristics and habits of a conscious relationship. These sections of the book can serve as a guide to make sure you don't fall into the same bad habits again.

You are capable of loving someone else and yourself at the same time. The two are not mutually exclusive. When you do this, your relationship won't feel so precarious anymore.

Your partner's happiness should be important to you, but it shouldn't be the center of your life. It should be one part of your life. Since you aren't with a narcissist anymore, your happiness should matter to them, too.

This applies to both of you: you can't rely on your partner alone to make you happy. You are each responsible for your own happiness. The relationship may sway your moods in one direction or the other, but if the state of the relationship is the main factor that determines how happy each of you are, this means you have gotten into a codependent relationship again.

When your partner and you are independent, you won't experience the same rush from getting their approval. But you shouldn't measure the strength of your relationship by how much excitement you get from them.

Excitement will still be a part of your love, but you shouldn't be going between excitement and instability.

You are each one part of each other's lives; you are not each other's whole lives. Once you come to make this your truth, you and your partner will be able to have a loving, sustainable relationship.

6.6 How to Deal with the Fear of Conflict

It's completely normal to be afraid of conflict. The problem arises when we avoid conflict as a rule, no matter how much it affects us.

The core of solving this problem is learning self-respect. If you have self-respect, you won't let people mistreat you. You will know that you can't always avoid conflict if you choose to be respected. This will come naturally to you when you feel secure in your identity and your self-worth.

You will know for sure that you are a valuable person, and the idea of someone mistreating you will fill you with righteous anger. You still won't be the kind of person who hurts others when they are angry, but you won't let people get away with disrespecting you either.

Avoiding conflict will no longer feel like a choice; you will not accept being mistreated. The fear of conflict will be totally extinguished by your knowledge that you deserve better.

But maybe it is hard for you to imagine yourself like that at the moment. It is completely fine if you do not see yourself this way right now — you will get there. What matters now is that you learn how to stop avoiding conflict in small steps.

You have to start small. When we are afraid of conflict, we envision the consequences of confronting someone to be terrible. This causes us to think that talking out the issue with someone would be intense and climactic.

But like a lot of our emotions, our fear of conflict makes us think the problem is something bigger than it is. You will have to get into the habit of acknowledging conflict in smaller situations, and then you will see that it is not so bad to put conflict out in the open.

A good way to start is when you order food. You don't have to make a scene out of it, but when your server brings you the wrong order, politely correct them. I know for a fact that many of the same personalities who end up with narcissists will avoid telling their server that they got the wrong order. It makes sense; staying with a narcissist and choosing not to correct the order both happen when a person doesn't want to draw attention to the conflict. It's admittedly a small step, but it's a small step that means something. When you correct the server, you will realize that they won't be mad at you, no one will look at you weird, and your food will be corrected.

Next step is to practice saying, "No." The word alone can be intimidating, but confronting conflict often requires it. In a real conflict, you want to follow "No" with something after it. "No, I would actually prefer if you didn't play music so loud." You can still sound polite, but the firm "No" at the beginning makes it clear that you are asserting yourself.

On the point of assertiveness, you need to stop saying phrases like "I'm sorry," "Please," "If that's OK," and so on.

Of course, there are situations where you want to be courteous, and you should keep saying these phrases. But in most casual social situations, these phrases signal to other people that you have a submissive personality.

I'm not telling you to change yourself completely. But it is a simple fact that the language you use tells people things about you.

You escaped the narcissist, but narcissists aren't the only kinds of people who will try to take advantage of you. You can know yourself to be a nurturing, passive person deep down, but you don't want to give strangers this impression. They will use you as a doormat.

Assertiveness is the key to confronting conflict. And it doesn't mean you have to be aggressive. If you want to be honest with someone about how they hurt you, you can tell them, "I respect you, but I want you to know how I feel."

It's direct, but not impolite. It may take some time for you to say something like this, but it's a goal you need to shoot for.

CHAPTER 7

AFFECTIVE DEPENDENCE HOW TO GET OUT OF IT IN 3 STRATEGIES

7.1 How to Get Out of a Relationship

Relationships with narcissists always involve affective dependence. Staying in this relationship for emotional fulfillment is short-term gratification: it works for a time, but it can't last. The best choice for you is to get out of a relationship of affective dependence.

Let us recall the difference between affective dependence and codependency.

Codependency is when someone in a relationship relies on their partner needing them. It makes them feel whole to know that someone else is relying on them.

Affective dependence is another feature of a relationship with a narcissist, but it is something else. It is when you get all your emotional needs from one person. Like all the features of this relationship, it is unstable. At the end of the day, it is impossible to get all your emotional needs met by one person.

All of us need people in our lives to feel whole. Affective dependence doesn't refer to needing love from our relationships; this is healthy and normal.

Affective dependence refers to using *one* person for all of these needs. It puts a heavy burden on that one person. When we glamorize relationships where each partner of a couple can't live without the other, we glamorize affective dependence.

Part of what kept you leaving them was your fear of not having your needs met when they were gone. If you hadn't expected them to be the sole thing that made you happy in the first place, this fear wouldn't hold you back. But since you convinced yourself that you needed them, you convinced yourself that their abuse was better than being alone.

Making yourself independent from the narcissist means feeling emotionally balanced without any other person.

People come and go; this is a fact of life. Other people are not a reliable way to feel happy.

The same idea goes for anything outside of yourself. Food can't make you happy; drugs and alcohol can't make you happy. They might work in the short term, but once your taste for them goes away, you are stuck with the same empty feeling.

Affective dependence might be the last thing that keeps you from leaving your partner. The fear of missing out on their company is very real; even when the objective reality is emotional abuse, we imagine that the alternative of loneliness couldn't be better.

That's why we are devoting an entire chapter to breaking out of this paradigm. You can, in fact, be happy with yourself and only yourself. You can, in fact, let go of this person. Once you have, you'll feel incredulous that you hadn't done so sooner.

You may think narcissist's companionship made you feel emotionally whole at least some of the time, but the only thing they succeeded in was distracting you.

The project of fixing them distracted you from facing yourself; the cycle between their rage and their bliss distracted you from facing yourself. A narcissist can't do the job of keeping you emotionally stable — not because he/she is a narcissist, but because no one can. The only reason you thought narcissists kept you stable was that they kept you so busy, you never had to deal with your emotions.

Distracting yourself from your emotions does not make them go away; they are always there, affecting everything you do.

This is why you blew up at the narcissist when you did. They never attended to your needs; they never saw you as a full person, so they never expected that you had so much bubbling underneath.

As you now understand that your partner alone can't make you happy, let's explore ways we can keep ourselves happy.

7.2 The Three Strategies

At least part of you knows that the narcissist is bad for your emotional health. But you stay, anyway, because you think they emotionally complete you. You think you wouldn't be complete if you were single.

Escaping affective dependence requires introspection. After you spend a lot of time examining your situation from the outside, you can see that this is not the case. Your partner doesn't do anything good for you emotionally; all they do is demean you. If they aren't demeaning you, they keep you busy trying to prevent this from happening next time.

You lose yourself giving them narcissistic supply and neglect yourself. You lose yourself so completely in the narcissist that you think ignoring your emotions is the same thing as being emotionally healthy.

Staying with a narcissist is a great way to hide from your emotions because they never give you a chance to think about yourself. You never have to acknowledge your own negative emotions because you are so busy with your partner's. You mistake losing yourself in someone else's life for emotional wellness.

The way narcissists absorb all of your attention is not something you should take lightly. They do such a good job of absorbing your attention that you don't even notice the emotions you are displaying.

The fact is, you are still displaying emotions when your life revolves around the narcissist. But your attention is so focused on your partner that you don't even realize it. People can tell that you aren't acting like yourself; they might ask you if you are doing all right. You are completely unaware that you are acting different, so you don't pick up on these things.

The narcissist notices, too. You may think you are doing a great job of hiding your frustration, but they can tell you aren't happy. This unleashes their rage even more because they can't understand why you would dare to be angry with them.

Clearly, being with such a person doesn't help your emotional stability. It makes you feel terrible and stressed, without even the benefit of knowing it.

A relationship with a narcissist won't make you feel whole, and neither will a relationship with a non-narcissist. You have to learn how to depend on yourself and yourself alone. Here are three strategies to accomplish this.

Reinforce Your Life

It means finding your center of gravity, recovering the centrality of your person regardless of who you have by your side.

Open your eyes to your tremendous power and potential. No matter who is next to you, you still have *you*. You are all you need because you are an amazing, intelligent human being.

I am not saying this to flatter you. What I mean is that all people have endless potential because of our ability to learn new things and adapt to new situations. Humans are the smartest things we know of, and you are no different. If you've ever been told that you are different in this regard, you can forget about their opinion just as you did with that of the narcissist. Every person is capable of so much more than they are aware of, and so are you. Embrace this fact, and you will realize that you don't need a partner to be happy.

Recall the exercise you did earlier in the book. I asked you to spend a few minutes with yourself and notice the thoughts that go through your head.

If you didn't do it before, try it now. The exercise asks very little of you: simply remove yourself from all people, devices, and sounds, and sit by yourself. Thoughts will run through your head. Don't worry about how unimportant your thoughts are or how unrelated they seem; just try to pay attention to what kinds of thoughts you have.

After doing this once, I want you to do it again, but take it a step further. Spend a few minutes alone with your thoughts and bring a notebook and pen with you. Don't write in it while you spend time with yourself, but have them ready in case you want to write down something you think of.

You can call this notebook your Identity Journal. As you practice doing this, you can change the activity to incorporate parts of your identity that you want to solidify. If you want to think of yourself as goal-oriented, you can try to have more thoughts about your goals and the steps you will take to achieve them. If you want to be more outgoing, think of people you know and how you could get to know them better.

As you do this activity, you will realize there is a lot more to you than you previously thought. There are a lot of things that your narcissistic ex didn't know about you; in fact, they barely knew you at all. Their idea of you was totally off. But your idea of yourself is richer than it ever was.

Avoid Negative Thoughts

Do away with the negative self-talk. The defeatist self-talk that goes through your head is self-fulfilling. I'm not saying you can just "turn it off" at will, but every time you have a negative thought, have a positive thought to go with it.

We don't know what the future holds, and your negative thoughts are only considering the negative possibilities. Consider the positive possibilities, too. You will end up with more realistic ideas of the world and yourself.

Recall the second part of the activity I gave you earlier in the book. I said that when you spend some time alone with your thoughts, you should insert some of your own positive thoughts to go with them.

I am still telling you to do the same thing now, but this time have your Identity Journal with you. If you think of a positive idea that particularly strikes you, write it down. As time passes, these positive thoughts will fill many pages.

You should feel free to write down your worries and concerns in the Identity Journal, too. But for each one, add two more positive thoughts. You can't forget that there are positive and negative possibilities for the future.

When you fill your head with the negative possibilities, your idea of the future is distorted, and it makes your present an unhappy one.

When You Want, at All Costs, the Partner, Do Learn to Reflect on the Uncontested Partner's Need for Fear of Being Alone

When you long to be with your exes, focus on how that benefits them. If you went back into their arms, you would be teaching them that their behavior is acceptable, and they will not change. They will not change, no matter what you do.

Don't play into their game because you are afraid of being alone. If you follow 1 and 2, you will gradually learn how to be happy alone for the time being. You won't have to accept it for long—after you heal, you will be ready to start dating again, and you will have a lot of life lessons under your belt.

CHAPTER 8

HOW TO EXIT A RELATIONSHIP OF CODEPENDENCE

(HEALING AND FORGIVENESS TRAUMA)

When you end the relationship with the "no contact" method, you will go through a period of pain. Since you were codependent for so long, it will take time to move on emotionally. After enough time passes, you will realize that life goes on without them, and things will start to feel normal again.

A codependent relationship is hard to leave because, on some level, you feel like you need permission from your partner to leave. Another part of you knows this isn't true, but the tension between these different sides of you creates a lot of confusion.

The first thing you need to understand is that you are an individual who has the right to protect themselves.

There will be a part of you that tries to delude yourself into thinking you don't have to leave them. That is why it is so important for you to look at the facts. If you keep making yourself aware of the facts, you will know that leaving them is what is really best for you. It will remind you that you don't need their permission because they won't give it to you. The fact that they have this much control over you is the entire problem.

You have to escape their control. The hardest part will be leaving because it requires you to lose some of the control they have over you and take ownership of your body in a way that you haven't in a long time.

Another thing that makes leaving them difficult is your brain likes what it knows; it likes what is familiar.

You will recall that one of the narcissist's recapture strategies is an appeal to the familiar. It is effective because we don't like the unknown. But sometimes, we have to embrace the unknown to protect ourselves. Your narcissistic partner is a dangerous known. It's true that you don't know what will come after breaking up with them, but you will have to face it. Take some comfort in the fact that with our guidance, you will know what to do next.

Leaving a codependent relationship fills our heads with so many contradictory feelings. We know that we are unhappy, but at the same time, we don't know how to leave. We don't know how to leave because the relationship has filled our entire consciousness for a very long time. It's almost as if we were in a state of hypnosis while we were with the narcissist.

This book has empowered you to take the one essential step to escape a codependent relationship, and that is to learn how to trust yourself.

Take time every day to do the exercises in your Identity Journal. Even if you haven't broken up with your partner yet, keep writing in it.

Your journal will remind you that you have reached a turning point. You are not going to keep living every day with this person as if it is normal.

It is also a reminder that making changes is a step-by-step process. You can't be too hard on yourself for taking the time to make such a big change. You should write in your journal the day that you are going to leave. Then, write what happens the next day, and the day after that.

You are well-equipped to reclaim your independence.

You might not expect me to say this, but a vital step in the healing process is to forgive the narcissist. I am not telling you to forget what they did and try to make it work — not at all. I am telling you to forgive them for your own benefit.

Once you can let go of how you suffered because of your ex, you will be ready to start the next phase of your life. Because of the "no contact" rule, don't forgive them in person. Forgive them privately. Think: "You hurt me in so many ways, but I'm ready to move on with my life. You are human just like me, and you made a lot of mistakes that caused me harm—but I'm not going to hold onto this anger against you forever. I forgive you."

You won't feel ready for this soon after the break-up, but keep forgiving them in the back of your mind. If you don't forgive them, you let them take up space in your head longer than they deserve.

Conclusion

Thank you for making it through to the end of *Disarm Narcissism and Codependency*! Let's hope it was informative and able to provide you with all of the tools you need to achieve your goals—whatever they may be.

I sincerely hope this book has helped you look at your relationship with a narcissist in a more objective way. Understanding the dynamics of codependent relationships and how narcissists try to keep them alive should awaken you to what you probably have to do next — end the relationship.

As a partner of a narcissist, you are undoubtedly a victim, but I hope I helped you see how your own patterns and personality traits contributed to the cycle of codependency. At the end of the day, the narcissist is the one who caused you to feel worthless and weak, so they are to blame for what you went through—not you. However, the only way out of this toxic relationship is to put a halt on your participation in it.

Recall the analogy we made between training dogs and teaching narcissists. The next time you and your partner go through a rough patch, don't teach them that you are swayed by their recapture strategies. Teach them that you have no response to them at all.

One of the most useful tips in this whole book is that narcissists can't stand indifference. They can feed off positive and negative attention alike, but if you pay them no mind at all, they will learn that they can't source narcissistic supply from you and move on.

This is especially important to remember when you do "no contact." They will try to contact you in every way possible, but if you act like you don't care, either way, the narcissist will realize you aren't useful to them anymore.

After you decisively put an end to the relationship, many thoughts will fly through your head. They will include thoughts of doubt and relief. Now that you can think about what your ex put you through more clearly, you will have space to focus on yourself. Once you are ready to date again, you will be able to spot a narcissist from a mile away. When that happens, run like hell.

Most importantly, you know that with a healthy sense of identity and self-worth, you can't be manipulated by narcissistic people ever again. The narcissist saw you as insecure and used it to their advantage.

You won't be vulnerable to the charms of a narcissist ever again because now, you know the forms they take. You also won't care about flattery because you will already know yourself. You won't need someone else to tell you if you are smart, beautiful, or anything else. You already know these things.

Sometimes, pain is necessary to feel. None of the pain that you went through when the narcissist put you down was necessary to feel, but the pain you feel from letting them go is necessary. They put you through a lot when you were together, and unfortunately, it is a fact that you will have to go through some more pain when you break up with them.

Ask yourself after you are through with them: do you care at all what your ex thinks about you? You will find that early on in the process of losing them, the answer will not be "No." That's the nature of the codependent relationship: you care so much about what your partner thinks of you. It's very hard to unlearn this.

But just like you will learn how to let them go, you will learn how to let go of what they think of you. Because of "no contact," you won't hear what they think of you, either. All the echoes of what they used to say will exist in your head and in your head alone. Over time, these echoes naturally fade.

The less you care about what your ex thinks of you, the further along you are in recovering yourself.

You already know yourself. Since the narcissist took so much out of you, you just weren't the center of your attention for a very long time. You can move on from that stage in your life now. When you realize how wonderful it is to be free of their demands, you will exhale deeply. It feels like you are a new person. But you aren't a new person — you just remembered about yourself again.

Your friends and family will be relieved that you aren't together, too. If you didn't tell them the truth about the relationship before, you could feel free to tell them about it now. They will understand why you weren't open to them. You will be surprised by how many people have had experiences with narcissists. They are like the flu that everyone has had. Once they are over it, they sure are glad it is over.

Now that you are near the end of the book, you are running out of excuses to stay in this toxic situation, if you still are. I have told you all the reasons your codependent and affectively dependent relationship doesn't work. I have told you how the narcissist trapped you and why they will never be able to love you.

You have the knowledge now. It's time to put it into action.

I warned you from the very beginning: the longer you allow yourself to stay in this situation, the harder it will be to get out of it. Everything that was in your life before this relationship will seem farther and farther away until the narcissist is the thing you know most. You don't want to reach this point.

The longer you spend around a person, the more of an effect they have on you. This means narcissists' spell becomes stronger the longer it takes for you to leave them. If you think it is hard for you to leave now, it will be even harder if you wait another month.

It will be hard to make this change, no matter how much time you give yourself. It will be hard today; it will be hard next week; it would have been hard last week. Timing isn't important. No matter when you do it, you have to resist everything your codependency is telling you to do and cut them off.

Abuse is never the fault of the victim, but sadly, we all have to defend ourselves in this world. An unwavering idea of who you are will protect you from all forms of psychological abuse. If you only got one thing from this book, I want it to be that. There are people who use mental and emotional tricks to exploit you, but if your mind's "self-concept" room has sturdy walls, narcissists will have no luck trying to tear them down.

Finally, if you found this book useful in any way, a review on Amazon is always appreciated!

CPSIA information can be obtained
at www.ICGtesting.com
Printed in the USA
BVHW060439250321
603396BV00004B/251